D0122181

HONG KONG'S TRANSITION
A DECADE AFTER THE DEAL

HONG KONG'S TRANSITION

A Decade After the Deal

Editors
Wang Gungwu
Wong Siu-lun

Contributors
Sze-yuen Chung, John C. C. Chan, Henry Litton,
George Shen, Rita Fan, Steven N. S. Cheung,
Ambrose Y. C. King, Louis Cha, Leung Chun-ying,
Christopher Patten

HONG KONG
OXFORD UNIVERSITY PRESS
OXFORD   NEW YORK
1995

Oxford University Press

Oxford New York
Athens Auckland Bangkok Bombay
Calcutta Cape Town Dar es Salaam Delhi
Florence Hong Kong Istanbul Karachi
Kuala Lumpur Madras Madrid Melbourne
Mexico City Nairobi Paris Singapore
Taipei Tokyo Toronto

and associated companies in
Berlin Ibadan

Oxford is a trade mark of Oxford University Press

First published 1995

Published in the United States
by Oxford University Press, New York

© *Oxford University Press 1995*

British Library Cataloguing in Publication Data
available

Library of Congress Cataloging-in-Publication Data

Hong Kong's transition : a decade after the deal / editors Wang
Gungwu, Wong Siu-lun ; contributors Sze-yuen Chung . . . [et al.].
p. cm.
A collection of ten lectures, held at the University of Hong Kong
from January 15 to April 14, 1994.
ISBN 0-19-587400-5
1. Hong Kong—Politics and government. 2. Hong Kong—Economic
conditions. 3. Hong Kong. I. Wang, Gungwu. II. Wong, Siu-lun.
III. Chung, S. Y. (Sze Yuen)
DS796.H757H64 1995
951.25—dc20 95–21156
CIP

Printed in Hong Kong
Published by Oxford University Press (China) Ltd
18/F Warwick House, Taikoo Place, 979 King's Road, Quarry Bay,
Hong Kong

Contents

Preface

IN 1984 the Chinese and British governments signed the Joint Declaration in which it was agreed that Hong Kong would cease to be a British colony and would revert to Chinese rule on 1 July 1997. A few months after the Sino-British Agreement was concluded, the University of Hong Kong held an academic conference on the subject. In that conference, policies and strategies for maintaining Hong Kong's prosperity and stability before and after 1997 were proposed and discussed. The proceedings were published afterwards in a volume entitled *Hong Kong and 1997: Strategies for the Future.*[1]

Now ten years have passed since the Joint Declaration was signed. There are just three more years to go before the transitional period will be over and Hong Kong will become a Special Administrative Region (SAR) of China. This is an appropriate time, we feel, for us to review what has happened within our community in the past decade, and to take stock of how the transition has fared so far. It is clearly too early for conclusions to be drawn, but it is not too soon for reflections. By taking time to look back, we should be able to go forward with a clearer sense of direction. It was in this spirit that we organized this series of Hong Kong Lectures. Instead of adopting the usual format of an academic conference, we decided to invite ten eminent speakers to address important aspects of the transition. They were chosen for their unique experience and expertise in particular areas of endeavour. We suggested the topics and asked each speaker to give a lecture for about an hour which would be followed by discussions with the audience. The lectures were held at the University of Hong Kong from 15 January to 14 April 1994. This book is a collection of the texts of those lectures, arranged in the sequence in which they were originally given.

[1] Y. C. Jao, C. K. Leung, P. Wesley-Smith, and S. L. Wong (eds), *Hong Kong and 1997: Strategies for the Future*, Hong Kong: University of Hong Kong, Centre of Asian Studies, 1985.

By design, each lecture is self-contained and has a focus of its own. It is worth noting, however, that several common themes recur which highlight distinct features of the transition. First, the speakers almost all agree that the events of 4 June 1989 in Tiananmen Square marked a watershed in the transition. Occurring in the middle of the ten-year transitional period, the incident left a deep scar in the minds of the Hong Kong people; it dealt a shattering blow to the Sino-British relationship, and it changed, in fundamental ways, the local political landscape.

However, the souring of political relationships was counterbalanced by the strengthening of economic bonds. The impressive transformation of the Chinese economy is the second theme emphasized by the speakers. In the past decade, Hong Kong entrepreneurs have taken the lead in relocating their industrial operations across the border. As a result of this massive movement, Hong Kong has become the major source of foreign investment in the People's Republic of China. There has been a reverse flow of funds from the Mainland into Hong Kong too, making China one of the largest external investors in the Territory. As a result, the economic boundary between Hong Kong and China has diminished, and the two economies are more interdependent than ever before.

This unanticipated economic development has contributed to the continuing prosperity of Hong Kong over the past ten years—the third theme running through the lectures. This increasing affluence—which was largely unforeseen—generated an internal momentum within the community and a desire for change. The Joint Declaration's formal guarantee that there would be no change to the local system and way of life has not led to social stagnation. Instead, since 1984, Hong Kong has made a determined effort to reform itself. The heated debate on the pace of democratization was striking, but it was only one amongst a whole range of reforms which were underway. Significant changes were introduced in various fields, such as law, education, the economy, health, and social welfare, which transformed the community but sustained its dynamism.

The fourth theme addressed by the speakers is the changing mood of the community in its preparation for 1997. The past decade has been an exciting and dramatic one, full of unexpected events and emotions. There was the early phase of relative harmony when the Basic Law was being drafted, followed by the fluctuations of the Sino-British relationship which reached an impasse during the aftermath of the June Fourth Incident. A new Governor arrived with a controversial constitutional proposal, creating fiery confrontation and political deadlock. The 'through train' idea was derailed politically.[2] The Preliminary Working Committee was set up by the Chinese government in order to build a new 'stove' in 1997.[3] Change is indeed the key motif of the past decade.

Finally, a note of caution resounds through the lectures, revealing hidden dangers, yet to be clearly identified and effectively tackled. Foremost amongst these dangers is the spectre of rising corruption both here in Hong Kong and across the border in mainland China. Besides corruption, there are also potential problems in law and order, economic productivity, inadequacies in social welfare provisions, growing public financial commitments, and in the relative lack of official expertise in conducting a relationship with China.

By its very nature, this collection of lectures cannot hope to be comprehensive. Omissions will doubtless exist. In terms of the range of topics covered, we are conscious that weighty issues, such as infrastructural development, environmental protection, immigration, and emigration, are missing. As for the variety of perspectives presented, our greatest regret was our inability to include the Chinese official view. Attempts were made to enlist as speakers Chinese officials closely involved in Hong Kong, but because of time constraints and other reasons, the officials concerned were not able to accept our invitation.

This book contains the first series of lectures. Its focus is

---

[2] The term 'through train' refers to the arrangement whereby those elected to the Legislative Council in 1995 would continue to serve until 1999, thus ensuring political continuity across the 1997 threshold.

[3] The Preliminary Working Committee (PWC) was set up in June 1993 when the Sino-British relationship deteriorated over Chris Patten's electoral proposals. Refusing to accept those proposals, China has announced its intention of establishing a new political structure or a 'second stove' in Hong Kong. One of the main tasks of the PWC is to provide advice on how to proceed.

on the development of Hong Kong itself over the past ten years. The second series of Hong Kong lectures, held between September and November 1994, dealt with the external relationship of Hong Kong and the regional role that it can play in the future. We plan to have this second series of lectures published in a volume which will form a sequel to this book.

The Hong Kong Lectures are made possible through the generous financial support of the Mrs Li Ka Shing Fund. We would like to thank Mr Rupert Chan, Director of the External Relations Office of the University of Hong Kong, and his staff. We would also like to thank Miss Vivian Wong, Secretary of the Li Ka Shing Distinguished Lectures Committee of the University, for her assistance in producing this series of Hong Kong Lectures. We are also grateful to Mrs Rosanna Lam, Mr Lau Wing Yat, Miss Leung Yuk Sim, and Mr Eric Tsang of the Department of Sociology at the University for preparing the manuscript for publication.

Wang Gungwu
Wong Siu-lun
Hong Kong, July 1994

Tables and Figures

Tables

Figures

Contributors

SZE-YUEN CHUNG has served on the Legislative Council since 1965 and as its Senior Member between 1974 to 1978. He became a member of the Executive Council in 1972 and was the Senior Member for eight years until 1988. First Knighted in 1978, he received his second Knighthood in 1989. He has held many prestigious public posts, including chairmanship of the Federation of Hong Kong Industries, the Hong Kong Productivity Council, Standing Commission on Civil Service Salaries, Hospital Authority, and Asian Productivity Organization. Sir Sze-yuen became a Hong Kong Affairs Adviser to the Chinese Government in 1992, and was appointed by them in 1993 to serve on the Preliminary Working Committee for the formation of Hong Kong's first Special Administrative Region (SAR) Government in July 1997.

JOHN CHO-CHAK CHAN is the former Secretary for Education and Manpower in the Hong Kong Government. A member of the civil service for a total of twenty-seven years (between 1964 and 1978, and 1980 and 1993), he rose through the ranks to become one of the few Cabinet-level Policy Secretaries. Among the key posts he has held over the years are those of Private Secretary to the Governor, Deputy Secretary (General Duties), Director of Information Services, Deputy Chief Secretary, and Secretary for Trade and Industry. He is now Managing Director of the Kowloon Motor Bus Company Limited.

HENRY LITTON is currently a Justice of Appeal. He is also Chairman of the Town Planning Appeal Board, a member of the Judicial Service Commission, Chairman of the Advisory Committee on Legal Education, a member of the Hong Kong University Council, and President of the Hong Kong Alliance Française. Born in Hong Kong, he started to practise as a barrister in 1960, and was appointed Queen's

Counsel in 1970. He founded the *Hong Kong Law Journal*, and served as its Editor-in-Chief for twenty-two years.

G EORGE SHEN, Chief Editor of the *Hong Kong Economic Journal*, is a specialist in productivity and economic development, with a particular interest in the Asia-Pacific region. From 1968 to 1986, before joining the *Journal*, he worked with the Asian Productivity Organization in Tokyo as Head of Administration and Public Relations. Between 1990 and 1992, Dr Shen served as a part-time member of the Central Policy Unit of the Hong Kong Government. His publications in English include *Productivity Measurement and Analysis* (1983) and *China's Investment in Hong Kong* (1993), whilst his Chinese publications include *Essays on China's Economy* (1989) and *Collection of Economic Essays* (1994).

R ITA FAN HSU LAI-TAI is the former Chairwoman of the Education Commission, and a past member of the Legislative and Executive Council in Hong Kong. She was Associate Director of the Hong Kong Polytechnic until 1990, Deputy General Manager of the Industrial Estates Corporation until 1992, and General Manager of the Emperor Group until 1994. She is now a member of the Preliminary Working Committee established by the Chinese Government, and the Vice-Chairwoman of the Hong Kong Federation of Women.

S TEVEN N. S. CHEUNG is Professor and Head of the School of Economics and Finance at the University of Hong Kong. He has previously taught at the California State College at Long Beach, the University of Chicago, and the University of Washington. He is editor of the *Asian Economic Journal*, and author of *The Theory of Shared Tenancy: With Special Application to Asian Agriculture and the First Phase of Taiwan Land Reform* (1969) and *Will China Go 'Capitalist'? An Economic Analysis of Property Rights and Institutional Change* (1982).

A MBROSE YEO-CHI KING is a Pro-Vice-Chancellor and Professor of Sociology at the Chinese University of Hong Kong. He has been a Visiting Fellow at the Centre of

International Studies at the Massachusetts Institute of Technology, and a Visiting Professor at the Universities of Wisconsin and Heidelberg; in 1994 he was elected Fellow of the Academia Sinica in Taiwan. In Hong Kong, he has held many advisory positions to the government, serving on the Independent Commission Against Corruption, and on the Law Reform Commission. His books include *From Tradition to Modernity: An Analysis of Chinese Society and Its Change* (1978), *The Politics of Three Chinese Societies* (1988), and *Salient Issues of Chinese Society and Culture* (1992).

L OUIS CHA was, until his recent retirement, founder and publisher of the *Ming Pao Daily News*, Hong Kong, *Shin Ming Daily News*, Singapore, and related publications. He is best known, however, as a writer, and is the most widely read novelist in Chinese communities all over the world. He was a member and co-convenor of the Political Structure Committee of the Drafting Committee of the Basic Law of the Hong Kong Special Administrative Region (1985–89). He is an Honorary Professor of the Universities of Hong Kong, British Columbia, Beijing, Zhejiang, and Hangzhou; he is an Honorary Fellow of St Antony's College and a Wynflete Fellow of Magdalen College, both in Oxford.

L EUNG CHUN-YING is former Secretary General of the Basic Law Consultative Committee, and Chairman and Managing Director of C. Y. Leung & Co Ltd—a regional real-estate consultancy with offices in nine Asian cities—which he founded in 1993. His public service includes membership of the Hong Kong Housing Authority, the Land Development Corporation, and the Airport Consultative Committee. He serves as Honorary Adviser on land reform to the Shanghai, Shenzhen, and Tianjin governments. As well as working as a Hong Kong Affairs Adviser, he has been appointed by the Chinese government as Co-convenor of the Political Sub-Group of the Preliminary Working Committee.

T HE RT HON CHRISTOPHER PATTEN has been Governor of Hong Kong since 1992. After graduating from Oxford, he joined the Conservative Research Department and became its youngest-ever director in 1974. Following the General Election of 1983, he served successively as Minister of State at the Department of Education and Science, Minister for Overseas Development at the Foreign and Commonwealth Office, and Secretary of State for the Environment. He was appointed to the Privy Council in 1989, and became Chancellor of the Duchy of Lancaster and Chairman of the Conservative Party in 1990. In 1983 he published his book, *The Tory Case*.

WANG GUNGWU is the Vice-Chancellor of the University of Hong Kong, and Emeritus Professor at the Australian National University in Canberra. Between 1990 and 1992 he served as a member of the Executive Council, and he is now Chairman of the Advisory Council on the Environment (formerly the Environmental Pollution Advisory Committee) in Hong Kong. His books include *China and the Chinese Overseas* (1991), and *The Chineseness of China* (1991).

WONG SIU-LUN is Professor of Sociology and former Director of the Social Sciences Research Centre at the University of Hong Kong. He is a Hong Kong Affairs Adviser, and a member of the Citizen Advisory Committee on Community Relations of the Independent Commission Against Corruption. He is the co-editor of *Hong Kong and 1997: Strategies for the Future* (1985), and the author of *Emigrant Entrepreneurs: Shanghai Industrialists in Hong Kong* (1988).

1 What Has Gone Wrong during the Transition?

SZE-YUEN CHUNG

Background to the Sino-British Diplomatic Negotiations

IN ORDER to appreciate the developments during the transition it is necessary to examine the background leading to the signing in 1984 of the Sino-British Joint Declaration on the Question of Hong Kong.[1] Whilst Hong Kong Island and the South Kowloon Peninsula were ceded to the British in the 1840s, the New Territories—covering 92 per cent of the whole of Hong Kong—were leased to Britain for ninety-nine years from 1898. Towards the end of the 1970s, not only the Hong Kong people, but also foreign investors, were becoming concerned about the political future of Hong Kong after 1997. In particular, there was increasing realization of the problem posed by individual land leases granted in the New Territories, all of which are set to expire three days before 30 June 1997.

During this period, the political scene in China was going through a major change. The 'Gang of Four', who were mainly responsible for the Cultural Revolution, had lost power, and Chairman Deng Xiaoping had re-emerged and taken over the control of the Chinese government. The Hong Kong people were impressed by his 'open door' policy for economic development.[2]

---

[1] The 'Joint Declaration of the Government of the United Kingdom of Great Britain and Northern Ireland and the Government of the People's Republic of China on the Question of Hong Kong' was signed in Beijing on 19 December 1984 by the Prime Ministers of the two countries. Britain agreed to return sovereignty of Hong Kong to China on 1 July 1997. China agreed to treat Hong Kong thereafter as a Special Administrative Region directly under the central government, with a high degree of autonomy and the maintainance of the current economic, social, and judicial systems, as well as the way of life.

[2] Towards the very end of the 1970s, Chairman Deng Xiaoping introduced a policy of economic reform and began to open up the Chinese economy to the outside world. This is generally referred to as Deng's 'open door' policy.

At the same time there was a growing body of opinion in Hong Kong that confidence would erode in the mid-1980s, if nothing was done to alleviate the uncertainty caused by the 1997 deadline. When the then Governor of Hong Kong, Lord MacLehose, visited Beijing in March 1979, an attempt was made to resolve the specific question of individual land leases in the New Territories expiring in June 1997. Unfortunately, these discussions not only did not result in any measures to relieve the concerns, but, in fact, created more speculations on Hong Kong's future.

In the course of the following two years there was increasing awareness of the need to remove the uncertainty which the 1997 deadline generated. At that time I was the Senior Unofficial Member of the Executive Council[3] and I publicly stressed the importance of this issue on the arrival ceremony of the new Governor, the late Sir Edward Youde, in May 1982.

The First Sino-British Duel on Hong Kong's Future

The British Prime Minister, Margaret Thatcher, visited Beijing in September 1982 for discussions with Chairman Deng Xiaoping. Although Mrs Thatcher failed to achieve her initial objective of persuading Chairman Deng to exchange Chinese sovereignty for British Administration after 1997, she, none the less, managed to get Chairman Deng to agree to enter into diplomatic talks on the future of Hong Kong with the common aim of maintaining the stability and prosperity of the Territory.

The Two Major Battles in the Negotiations

The first battle was similar to the argument about the chicken and the egg—which should come first? At the beginning of the diplomatic negotiations, the British insisted that agreement should first be reached on administrative arrangements for Hong Kong, which would guarantee its future prosperity

---

[3] The Hong Kong Executive Council consists of government officials (known as official members) and non-government members (known as unofficial members). The Senior Unofficial Member is the leader of the non-government members.

and stability, prior to discussing the issue of reverting to China sovereignty over the whole of Hong Kong. This was not acceptable to the Chinese who maintained that the British should first concede both sovereignty and administration. There was deadlock in the talks for almost a year, until October 1983, when the British government eventually made the concession in order to enable the talks to proceed.

As one battle came to an end, another began. This was the issue of the form of the agreement. The Chinese were not prepared to sign a treaty with the British, but rather wished to declare their 'policy objectives' for Hong Kong themselves.[4] The Chinese insisted that their policies towards Hong Kong after 1997 should be solely their own and did not need British endorsement. After haggling for a couple of months, the British finally accepted the Chinese argument and hence the title 'Sino-British Joint Declaration'.

Public Proclamation on the End of British Rule

In April 1984 the two governments completed initial discussions of the major issues and it became clear that an agreement would be possible. The British Foreign Secretary, Sir Geoffrey Howe, came to Hong Kong after his visit to China and, on 20 April 1984, disclosed at a special Legislative Council meeting the progress of the talks. He said that British sovereignty and administration over the whole of Hong Kong would end on 30 June 1997 and that the two governments would continue to examine arrangements which would enable Hong Kong, after 1997, to have a high degree of autonomy and to preserve its way of life, together with the essentials of the present system.

The Public Role of UMELCO during the Negotiations

After the British government's concession on Hong Kong sovereignty, the Unofficial Members of the Executive and Legislative

---

[4] Policy objectives are those basic policies of the People's Republic of China designed to maintain Hong Kong's prosperity and stability after 1997.

Councils (UMELCO) felt that the time had come for them to influence publicly both the British and Chinese governments. They hoped to obtain an arrangement that would maintain the stability and prosperity as well as the way of life in Hong Kong after the transfer of sovereignty in June 1997.

Their first major public activity was to send a delegation to London with the aim of reflecting the views of the Hong Kong people to members of the British Parliament prior to their debate on Hong Kong in the House of Commons of 14 May 1984. The first meeting of the delegation was with the All Party Hong Kong and China Group,[5] and it was conducted in a very unsympathetic atmosphere. The MPs and Lords present at the meeting were pointedly critical and expressed doubts regarding the validity of the views both reflected by members of the delegation and expressed in the UMELCO Position Paper published in Hong Kong on 9 May 1984.[6]

The proceedings of the meeting, when promptly reported by the media, produced an immediate response from the people of Hong Kong. Within hours, hundreds of supportive telex messages were received by the delegation in London, and, during the following few days, the UMELCO office in Hong Kong received messages of support from more than 8,000 individuals, about 1,500 organizations, and fifteen District Boards.

UMELCO Contact with the Xinhua News Agency

The new Director of the Xinhua News Agency,[7] Mr Xu Jiatun, arrived in Hong Kong in July 1983. UMELCO's first contact with him was at a dinner on 5 August 1983, especially arranged by Professor Ma Lin at his vice-chancellor's Lodge.[8] Since

[5] A group of members of both the Upper and Lower Houses of the British Parliament with interest in Hong Kong and China affairs.

[6] The UMELCO Position Paper was an attempt by the unofficial members of the Executive and Legislative Councils to reflect the views of the people of Hong Kong about the 1997 takeover.

[7] The Xinhua News Agency is the People's Republic of China's official national news agency. Its office in Hong Kong has become China's *de facto* consulate in the Territory.

[8] Professor Ma Lin is Vice-Chancellor of the Chinese University of Hong Kong and has a close relationship with officials of the Xinhua News Agency in Hong Kong.

then, together with Sir Q. W. Lee and occasionally with Baroness Dunn, we had been in regular secret contact with him.[9] In early 1984 it was agreed that UMELCO would visit Beijing in order to meet the Chinese leaders and convey the views of the Hong Kong people. We had been waiting for a date from Mr Xu for some time, but when, on 7 May, mid-May was suggested, we were unable to go; we had already decided and announced the UMELCO visit to London in the middle of that month.

It was for this reason that UMELCO went to London before going to Beijing, and this purely coincidental sequence of events appeared to cause some resentment on the part of the Chinese. We also believed that the Chinese government was not happy with some of the points made in the UMELCO Position Paper published on 9 May 1984, the date of departure for the UMELCO delegation to London.

The UMELCO Visit to Beijing

Quiet negotiations for a number of UMELCO members to visit Beijing continued with Mr Xu after the UMELCO delegation returned from London. It was suggested that the Senior Unofficial Members of both the Executive and Legislative Councils should be included, but Mr Xu, without giving any reason, refused to extend an invitation to the Senior Unofficial Member of the Legislative Council, Sir Roger Lobo, who is Portuguese by origin.

The three UMELCO members eventually left for the Chinese capital on 21 June 1984 intending to express the concerns of the Hong Kong people to Chairman Deng and other senior Chinese officials. Apart from reflecting the feelings of the local community, the three UMELCO members also made three specific recommendations for improving the Hong Kong people's confidence in the return to Chinese sovereignty. The first recommendation stated that for the people of Hong Kong to accept the Sino-British Agreement, the Agreement:

(1) must provide clear and precise definitions of all aspects of Hong Kong's existing systems;

[9] Both Sir Q. W. Lee and Baroness Dunn were at that time Unofficial Members of the Executive Council. Regular secret meetings were held at third party locations in order to avoid the notice of the media.

(2) must be mutually binding as between the two signing governments; and

(3) must contain a provision stipulating that the Basic
Law of the Special Administrative Region will be
based on the terms in the Agreement.

The second recommendation was that the Basic Law should
be drafted in Hong Kong by the people of Hong Kong, together with representatives from Beijing and approved by the
Standing Committee of the National People's Congress (NPC).[10]
The third was the establishment by the Chinese government
of a Committee consisting of Chinese people of international
standing and reputation who would monitor the implementation and subsequent amendment of the Basic Law after 1997.

At that time the Chinese leaders accepted the first recommendation and said that they would consider the other two
after the signing of the Agreement. It is now common knowledge that the Sino-British Joint Declaration, particularly
its Annex I, was very detailed, and that sub-paragraph (12)
of Paragraph 3 contained a commitment by the Chinese government to reflect the relevant terms of the Joint Declaration in the Hong Kong SAR Basic Law. It is also on record
that about half of the members of the Basic Law Drafting
Committee were Hong Kong people.

As to the third recommendation, on 4 April 1990, the
Chinese National People's Congress approved the formation
of the Committee for the Hong Kong SAR Basic Law to assist
the Standing Committee of the NPC in the implementation
and amendment of the Basic Law after 1997.

The Honeymoon in the Post-Joint Declaration Period

The signing of the Sino-British Joint Declaration heralded
twelve and a half years of transition. These years, in my view,
could be classified into three distinct periods each with a
particular characteristic of its own.

The first period—from January 1985 to June 1989—could
be regarded as 'the period of cooperation'. This was the honey-

---

[10] The Standing Committee will act on behalf of the NPC between its Annual
Plenary Sessions.

moon period after the signing of the Joint Declaration. The British and the Hong Kong governments on the one side and the Chinese government on the other, appeared to be friendly and cooperative. There was good progress in the work of the Sino-British Joint Liaison Group, and good communication between the two governments.

The Drafting of the Hong Kong SAR Basic Law

The mammoth task of drafting the Basic Law for the Hong Kong SAR began in July 1985 when the Chinese government appointed the Basic Law Drafting Committee. About half of the fifty-nine members were Hong Kong people. Subsequently, a Basic Law Consultative Committee—consisting of over a hundred members and covering almost every walk of life in Hong Kong—was formed by the Chinese government to assist in the important work of the Drafting Committee.

The most difficult work in the drafting of the Basic Law was the design of the political system for the Hong Kong SAR. The reason for this was that the Chinese government had already declared in the Sino-British Joint Declaration that the current social, judicial, financial, and economic systems, as well as the lifestyle in Hong Kong, would remain unchanged; and that the laws currently in force in Hong Kong would remain basically the same. The job of the Drafting Committee was to transcribe these current systems into the Basic Law.

However, this was not to be the case for the political system of the Hong Kong SAR. The Chinese had laid down in Annex I of the Joint Declaration the principal structure of the Hong Kong SAR government and the method of its formation. First, it stated that there was to be a Chief Executive, selected by election or through consultations held locally and appointed by the Central People's government. This Chief Executive was to replace the current Governor appointed with no local consultation by the British Prime Minister in London. Principal officials of the Hong Kong SAR would be nominated by the Chief Executive and appointed by the Central People's government.

The Joint Declaration also stated that the legislature of the Hong Kong SAR would be constituted by elections instead of by appointment by the Governor—the traditional method in British colonies. However, there was no mention of the structure of the legislature, nor the methods to be used in the elections.

The Design of the Hong Kong SAR Political System

As the Chief Executive and the legislature were to be separately selected or elected, the Hong Kong SAR political structure was likely to be more akin to the American system than the British Westminster style. None the less, in 1984 it was still not clear whether or not the Hong Kong SAR government would follow more closely the American practice, which has the following additional and important features:

(1) The complete separation of power among the three government branches of executive, legislative, and judiciary, so that no one can be a member of more than one branch of the government at any one time.

(2) The President, Senate, and House of Representatives would be elected by different constituencies for terms of different lengths and at different times.

The Drafting Committee therefore had the difficult task of deciding on a detailed arrangement of the Hong Kong SAR political system, which would maintain Hong Kong's prosperity and stability after 1997.

The Importance of Sino-British Cooperation on the Development of Hong Kong's Political System during the Transition

In my view, the most important problem in the transition has been the cooperation of the two governments on the development of the political system for the Hong Kong SAR. It would have been disastrous if both governments had proceeded separately without mutual understanding. The objective must be for the two systems to converge on 1 July 1997. The Hong Kong government has stated from time to time that it intends to take a step-by-step approach in the reform of the legislature.

The first step was taken in the October 1985 elections, when the Hong Kong people had their first taste of limited democracy. Twenty-four members—42 per cent of the legislature—were elected through a system of functional and electoral college constituencies.[11] During the following three years, until October 1988, the new-style Legislative Council, made up of twenty-four elected members and twenty-two appointed ones, together with ten official members, functioned well, despite their diverse backgrounds and stances.

Further Development of the Hong Kong SAR Representative Government

In May 1987, a Green Paper[12] entitled 'The 1987 Review of Developments in Representative Government' was published by the Hong Kong government in order to discover the views of the community on future political developments. It received unprecedented response from the public with over 130,000 written submissions. As a result, the following February, the government published a White Paper[13] entitled 'The Development of Representative Government: The Way Forward'.

This important White Paper set out the Hong Kong government's plans for the next stage in the development of representative government and contained a number of major decisions in relation to elections for the Legislative Council. In particular, these decisions included the introduction of ten directly elected seats in the 1991 elections, and the composition and presidency of the Legislative Council. The White Paper also enshrined the four major objectives of the Hong Kong government, one of which was that the political

[11] Functional and electoral college constituencies are two different forms of indirect election. Functional constituencies are basically occupational groupings in business, industry, and professions. The electoral college constituency comprises all elected and appointed members of District Boards in the Territory.

[12] A consultative document published by the Hong Kong government to seek the views and opinions of the local population on certain important issues.

[13] A policy document published by the Hong Kong government on certain important issues as a result of the preceding Green Paper.

system in place before 1997 should permit a smooth transition in 1997 and a high degree of continuity thereafter. It is therefore difficult to dispute the claim made by the Chinese in 1992 and 1993 that the British and Hong Kong governments had broken their 1988 promise to develop the Hong Kong political system during the transition period in such a way that it would converge smoothly with the SAR Basic Law in 1997.

During the same period, the Basic Law Drafting Committee was making good progress, and, in April 1988, it published its first draft of the Basic Law for public consultation. Resulting from these public debates and consultations, a second draft Basic Law, with more than one hundred amendments on the first draft, was published in February 1989 for further public consultation.

The Tiananmen Square Incident Leading to the Period of Suspicion

Whilst the Hong Kong public were in the midst of deliberating the second draft Basic Law, a major development occurred in China in May 1989. Following the death in April of the Secretary-General of the Communist Party, Hu Yaobang, university students demonstrated in Beijing's Tiananmen Square. They were seeking a dialogue with the government with a view to stamping out corruption in the administration and to introducing greater democracy. Many Hong Kong people were sympathetic towards the students, and the first of a series of mass rallies in Hong Kong took place on 18 May 1989.

On 4 June, rallies attended by over one million Hong Kong people were held to express sorrow at the tragic events in Beijing. These events, which appeared on the local Hong Kong television every day for about two months, had a traumatic effect on its people. About half of the local population had already had personal experience of communist rule. Confidence in Hong Kong was badly shaken and people became more nervous about their future. This was the beginning of 'the period of suspicion' during the transition.

The Involvement of OMELCO

Most of the members of both the Executive and Legislative Councils shared the concern of the Hong Kong people. They decided to promote two major campaigns as a means to restore confidence. First, they requested the British government to give 'right of abode' in the United Kingdom to the 3.25 million British Dependent Territory Citizens in Hong Kong. An OMELCO[14] delegation was despatched in June 1989 to London to lobby the British government and Members of Parliament.

The second OMELCO campaign was to seek a much faster rate of political development, and, in particular, a much larger number of directly elected seats in the Legislative Council. It was suggested that there should be thirty directly elected Members (instead of ten as stipulated in the 1988 White Paper) for the 1991 elections, and that by 1995 the whole legislature should be constituted by universal suffrage. The two Senior Members of OMELCO, Baroness Dunn and Allen Lee, went to London in early 1990 to persuade the British government to accept the OMELCO model.

The OMELCO Gamble

Intensive efforts were exerted by members of OMELCO to seek support for their ideas. I had retired almost a year before that time from my Senior Unofficial Member post in the Executive Council, but, despite this, they still sought me out for support. I remember vividly my long discussion of over two hours with the then two Senior Members of OMELCO, at the Mandarin Hotel on 5 July 1989.

I drew their attention to the fact that the neutrality of the Hong Kong government and people towards domestic politics in China had been a major contributing factor to Hong Kong's prosperity and stability since 1950. My view was that this situation should not change as a result of the signing in 1984 of the Sino-British Joint Declaration on the Question of Hong Kong. The reason was very obvious. Once

---

[14] OMELCO stands for Office of the Members of the Executive and Legislative Councils. It provides support for the forty non-official members of the two Councils.

Hong Kong began taking sides in Chinese domestic politics, it would become a player in the game and be involved in the gamble. At the end of the game, Hong Kong would be either a winner or a loser. Those Hong Kong people who could emigrate to other countries could probably take the chance, but the great majority of the local residents would have to stay behind after 1997, and could not afford to lose. The discussion eventually ended in an agreement to disagree.

The Apparent Change of the British and Hong Kong Governments' Position on Neutrality

During this crucial period in 1989, whilst some associations were conducting mass campaigns in support of the student movement in Beijing, the Hong Kong government showed signs of change in its policy of neutrality towards Chinese domestic politics. Notorious anti-China elements from the West were allowed to enter Hong Kong for the first time since the 1950s to organize and conduct activities which the Chinese government would consider subversive. These events gave the Chinese government reasons for resentment and suspicion.

Concurrently, the British government was putting pressure on the Chinese to increase the number of directly elected seats in the Legislature in the 1991 election. They wanted more than the number suggested in the Hong Kong government's own 1988 White Paper, and by the 1995 election, more than the number in the second draft Basic Law. In February 1990, the Chinese agreed to speed up the pace of direct election in Hong Kong from fifteen seats to twenty in 1997, and they did not object to the Hong Kong government's raising the number of directly elected members in the 1991 elections from the ten—as stipulated in the 1988 White Paper—to eighteen.

At that time, the work of the Hong Kong SAR Basic Law Drafting Committee was in its final stage. It is now public knowledge that both the British and Chinese governments conducted secret negotiations in January 1990 and came to an understanding regarding the political system enshrined in the Basic Law. When the Hong Kong SAR Basic Law was promulgated by the Chinese government in April 1990, both the British government and the House of Commons issued statements hailing its contents. It was natural, I feel, for the Chinese to show their frustration and indignation when the British government later supported some Hong Kong people who called for the amendment of the Basic Law.

The Changing Political Scene in Eastern Europe

During 1989 and 1991 there were major and rather unexpected political developments in Eastern Europe which caused Western countries to reshape their foreign policies. With the integration of East and West Germany and the disintegration of the USSR, China is now the only major communist regime in the world.

The tripartite balance of world power has now changed to a bipartite confrontation between China and the United States. This political change probably stimulated the British government to do more for the protection of liberty and freedom in Hong Kong after 1997.

Margaret Thatcher in her memoirs, *The Downing Street Years*, recalls her thoughts during 1990, her last year as British Prime Minister. She states that the British government was brought under strong pressure that year to accelerate the process of democratization in Hong Kong. However, all her instincts told her that the time was not right. The Chinese leadership, she believed, was feeling acutely nervous and such a step at that moment could have provoked a strong defensive reaction which might have undermined the Sino-British Joint Declaration. She concluded that the British government needed to wait for calmer times before moving towards faster democratization. Is this Thatcher strategy responsible for the present-day confrontation between the British and Chinese governments on the 1995 Legislative Council elections?

British Citizenship and the Bill of Rights

The OMELCO lobby for the right of abode in Britain for the 3.25 million British subjects in Hong Kong achieved limited success. The British government in 1990 agreed to grant 50,000 families in Hong Kong full British Citizenship with the right of abode in the United Kingdom. The Chinese government was very uncomfortable with this British move, but could do nothing about it.

In addition to the granting of British Citizenship, the Hong Kong government continued to take certain measures to protect liberty and freedom, despite the fact that they might erode the mutual trust with China. A draft Bill of Rights to give effect to the provisions of the International Covenant on Civil and Political Rights was gazetted in March 1990 and thereafter passed into law. The Chinese government went on record to say that this particular law would be repealed after 1997.

The New Airport Development Scheme

The story of the airport development scheme might be considered as a typical example of the uncooperative attitude between the two governments during this period of suspicion. In October 1989, when the Hong Kong government first announced its plans for the massive airport development costing well over HK$100 billion, there had been no prior consultation with the Chinese government. It was thought that the project would be completed before the transfer of sovereignty in July 1997 and sufficient financial support would be forthcoming from investors and banks in the private sector. It was therefore not considered necessary to seek Chinese endorsement.

However, this view was not shared by those banks and financial houses who were potential providers of loans for the project: whilst the airport construction would be completed by 1997, the loans for the project would not be repaid until well after this date. The potential financiers needed a Chinese endorsement on the project, and it was only when this became clear that the two governments entered into discussion of the project. Apparently, because of this sequence of events, the Chinese were not very co-operative; the negotiations had a bad start and progress was very slow.

Memorandum of Understanding Concerning the Airport Project

With the aim of speeding up the negotiation, the Foreign Policy Adviser to the British Prime Minister[15] visited Beijing during June and July 1991, and held a series of meetings on the airport project with Chinese government officials. As a result, agreement was reached and a Memorandum of Understanding (MOU) concerning the construction of the new airport in Hong Kong and related questions was initialled on 30 June and published four days later. The MOU was eventually signed in Beijing by the two Prime Ministers on 3 September 1991. It was thought at that time that the matter was amicably resolved and that the Hong Kong government could proceed with the construction of the new airport at Chek Lap Kok. This, unfortunately, was not the case. It is a long story. Let me explain.

At the beginning of the negotiations, the Chinese government was given a figure of HK$112 billion (at March 1991 price) and HK$164 billion (on a money-of-the-day basis) for the airport project's costs, and a figure of HK$5 billion for the fiscal reserve of the Hong Kong government on 30 June 1997.[16] It was only after a long period of hard bargaining that the British raised the fiscal reserve to HK$25 billion. It was also agreed that the Hong Kong government would be free to borrow as long as the total debt to be repaid after 30 June 1997 would not exceed HK$5 billion.

The Frustration of the Chinese

In March 1992, six months after the signing of the MOU, the Hong Kong government made public its estimated fiscal reserve on 30 June 1997. It was HK$78 billion—three times that stated in the MOU. At the same time, the Chinese government was informed that the cost of the whole project, also at March 1991 prices, had gone up by 14 per cent; the cost of the airport railway alone had risen by 85 per cent. The Chinese felt that they had been cheated.

[15] The Foreign Policy Adviser at that time (1991) was Sir Percy Cradock.
[16] The fiscal reserve is made up of the accumulated surpluses of income over expenditure over the years.

In the meantime, John Major, the British Prime Minister, announced the forthcoming change of the Hong Kong Governor, and there were rumours that the next Governor would be a person who would deal with the Chinese government in a more forceful manner. These rumours presumably caused the Chinese great concern, and resulted in their using the airport issue as a bargaining chip.

The Period of Confrontation

Christopher Patten, the new Governor of Hong Kong arrived in July 1992 and, after a two-month period of preparation, returned to London to seek an endorsement from the Prime Minister and the Foreign and Commonwealth Secretary, Douglas Hurd, of his proposal on the 1995 Legislative Council elections and the new arrangement for the Executive Council. The Governor's proposed package of political development was publicly hailed by the British Foreign and Commonwealth Secretary as very skillful. In the meantime, the Chinese were eagerly awaiting an opportunity to discuss the issue with the new Governor.

It is understood that on 26 September 1992 the British Ambassador in Beijing delivered to the Chinese Foreign Ministry an advance copy of the Governor's draft Annual Address to the Legislative Council. It is also understood that the Chinese were shocked by the portion relating to the formation of the Legislative Council in 1995, and they immediately requested the British government to withhold the announcement pending further discussion. The British agreed to discuss with the Chinese, but only after the Governor had delivered his Address on 7 October. This was the beginning of 'the period of confrontation'.

The Chinese government had first refused to negotiate with Britain unless the Governor of Hong Kong withdrew his proposed political package on the 1994/95 elections. None the less, the Chinese government eventually agreed in March 1993 to enter into diplomatic talks with the British government.

The British proposed political package basically consisted of five new major features in the 1994 election for the District Boards and the two Municipal Councils, and the 1995 election for the Legislative Council. These features were:

(1)   The voting age would be lowered from 21 to 18 years.
(2)   The voting method would be changed to single-seat, single-vote for each constituency of direct election.
(3)   All appointed seats in the District Boards and the two Municipal Councils would be abolished.
(4)   The formation of the nine new functional constituencies would be fundamentally different from the existing twenty-one constituencies. These nine new functional constituencies would cover almost 2.7 million voters and would in fact be a form of direct election.
(5)   The composition of the Election Committee for the ten seats in the Legislature will be composed solely of elected District Board Members.

The Chinese strongly opposed the composition of the Election Committee because they claimed that the British had broken the mutual understanding as evidenced by the published exchange of letters between the Foreign Ministers of the two countries in January and February 1990.

The Chinese also objected to the structure of the nine new functional constituencies which would violate the original concept of the functional constituency as previously promoted by the Hong Kong government itself. They were sympathetic to the majority view of the chairmen and members of the eighteen District Boards and the two Municipal Councils to retain the appointment system for these bodies.

The Chinese apparently had no objection to the lowering of the voting age to 18 years, since the voting age in China is the same.

The Chinese have not yet expressed their reaction on the voting method, but it is believed that they have reservations about the single-seat, single-vote system. As far as election of the legislature is concerned, the Chinese appear to prefer another voting method which is supposed to be more suitable for the future Executive-led political system in the Hong Kong SAR.

After seventeen rounds of talks spread over six months, the two sides have still failed to reach even an intermediate stage agreement, and the diplomatic negotiations eventually broke down in December 1993.

The British Hong Kong government have now [January 1994] tabled at the Legislative Council a Bill covering the partial political package. The Chinese, on the other hand, have announced that they will not recognize the elections organized by the British Hong Kong government in 1994 and 1995, and that they will hold fresh elections after the transfer of sovereignty on 1 July 1997. The Chinese government also established, in July 1993, a Preliminary Working Committee headed by the Chinese Vice-Premier and Foreign Minister to advise the Chinese government on the strategies, policies, and plans for a smooth transfer of sovereignty in 1997.

Both governments are engaged in 'megaphone diplomacy'[17] and there is no sign of a truce. When two parents argue, the victims are usually their children. In this case, the Hong Kong people will eventually be the true losers.

---

[17] Terminology used by the media in Hong Kong to describe the exchange of accusation by the British and the Chinese governments through the media.

2 The Civil Service: Continuity and Change

JOHN C. C. CHAN

THIS YEAR marks the tenth anniversary of the signature of the Sino-British Joint Declaration. In itself this is of no particular significance: what is far more important is that we now have less than three years to go—1,255 days to be exact—before sovereignty over Hong Kong is returned to China on 1 July 1997. Nevertheless, it provides a convenient occasion on which to take stock of how the transition has evolved so far, and to see what lessons, if any, can be drawn for the future. Clearly the transition has been nowhere near as smooth as we had hoped. Clearly, too, the people of Hong Kong are deeply concerned about the rest of the transitional period, and about what will be in place by 30 June 1997 to ensure full and proper implementation of the Joint Declaration.

It would not be an exaggeration to say that an absolutely essential ingredient for a smooth transition is the continuity of the Hong Kong civil service.

In this lecture, I intend to review the development of the civil service over the past ten years. I believe I am well placed to do this. I have been a civil servant for a total of twenty-seven years, and have seen a lot of the civil service from the inside. I have also had the opportunity to see it from the outside, and am doing so again now, with a certain degree of detachment (but admittedly not with complete impartiality).[1] I can therefore offer you my personal views and perceptions, based to a large extent on my personal experience and observations. I must, however, enter three caveats. First, as a retired civil servant—and technically still a civil servant until 4 May 1994—I am bound by the Official Secrets Acts and internal government regulations. I must be very careful not to breach any rule of confidentiality. Second, I wish to

---

[1] See John Chan's biography at the front of this book for details of his career inside and outside the civil service.

stress that the views I express are entirely personal and not necessarily representative of those of the Hong Kong government, not to mention Kowloon Motor Bus. Nor do I claim to be speaking on behalf of my former colleagues in the civil service, or even necessarily reflecting their views. Finally, the views I express do not reflect the reasons for my decision to retire early from the civil service and should not be interpreted as such. On that issue, I intend to continue to exercise my right of silence.[2]

A Definition of the Civil Service

What do we mean by the civil service? In Hong Kong, the process of government or public administration extends well beyond what I would call the civil service. There is an elaborate system of public consultation on, and participation in, government affairs. There are some 400 boards and committees of various kinds—mostly advisory in nature—covering virtually all areas of government activity. Even the Governor's inner cabinet, the Executive Council, consists of more people from outside the civil service than from within.[3] Many in the audience, I am sure, will have heard of or participated in one or more of these boards and committees. In addition, there are the institutions of representative government: the District Boards, the Municipal Councils, and the Legislative Council. There is also a large number of quasi-government organizations which may be wholly or partly funded by the government, but which are run autonomously by people who are outside the civil service.[4] Finally, there is an increasing number of statutory bodies which have very specific executive functions and which have the authority to engage their own staff—people who do not belong to what I would call the civil service.[5]

[2] John Chan's premature retirement from the civil service was the subject of intense speculation among the Hong Kong media. Mr Chan stated that he had decided to retire for 'personal reasons', but he did not elaborate.

[3] On 22 January 1994, the date this lecture was delivered, the Executive Council consisted of the Governor (as President), five civil servants, and nine other Members appointed by the Governor from outside the civil service.

[4] Examples include the Hong Kong Trade Development Council, the Hong Kong Productivity Council, and the Vocational Training Council.

[5] Examples include the Housing Authority, the Hospital Authority, and the Provisional Airport Authority.

My definition of the civil service would be that collection of individuals who are employed directly by the government, whose salaries and fringe benefits are paid out of public funds (or, more specifically, out of the 'Personal Emoluments' subheads of the various heads of expenditure in the government's budget) and whose employment and terms and conditions of service are subject to Civil Service Regulations.[6]

Role of the Civil Service in Hong Kong

Before we review the development of the civil service over the last ten years, let us look quickly at the role which the civil service performs. Naturally that role has been evolving and changing over the years, but its essence has remained basically unchanged.

Traditionally, Hong Kong has a government run by civil servants, rather than by elected politicians. Their mandate to govern derives from appointment by the Governor who is himself appointed by the Queen on the advice of the British government of the day. Hong Kong civil servants are functionaries operating in an apolitical and impartial manner, and most of them see the civil service as a profession and a life-long career.

Hong Kong has always enjoyed a high degree of autonomy. Relatively little is determined from the United Kingdom. All the decisions concerning the day-to-day affairs of Hong Kong are taken in Hong Kong, mainly by career civil servants who are expected to, and generally do, act in accordance with their conscience and their best judgment as to where the public interest lies. Because we do not have an elected government, there is a great deal of consultation and consensus-building—or consensus-seeking—in the process of government. This is where the very elaborate system of consultative bodies comes in.

However, whilst the process of government is characterized by an attempt to seek consensus through consultation, traditionally it is the civil service which takes a firm lead. Until the middle of the 1980s, all members of the Executive Council and the Legislative Council were appointed by the

[6] These are the internal administrative Regulations of the Hong Kong Government.

Governor. Indeed, originally, these bodies were largely composed of civil servants, but their proportion was progressively
reduced over the years, whilst the proportion of people from
outside the civil service was increased; nowadays, the non-
officials (as they used to be called) outnumber the officials.
But whilst the members of these bodies were men and women
of independent mind who were not obliged in any way to
accept, or even publicly to defend, proposals put forward by
the civil service, in practice the Governor and his team of civil
servants were generally able to carry the Councils and the
community along with them, and had relatively little trouble
in getting their policy proposals agreed and implemented.

On the face of it, the situation has changed very significantly in the last ten years. There is now much more public
debate on government policies and measures, a much sharper division of views and much more vocal dissent and criticism. The initiative seems increasingly to have left the hands
of civil servants, who no longer appear to be calling the
shots. Civil servants are often cast, or perceived to be, in the
role of the beleaguered public whipping-boy—trying very
hard, and perhaps not always successfully, to explain and
sell unpopular policies and decisions—rather than the traditional powerful mandarins to whom people pay homage. The
government is often perceived and criticized as being somewhat rudderless and uncertain of its own ground. Members
of the Legislative Council and of the other political bodies—
the District Boards, the Municipal Councils, and various fledg-
ling political parties—appear to be gaining the upper hand
as well as the centre stage.

Changes in the Operating Environment

These changed perceptions have been both the cause and
the effect of changes in the environment in which the civil
service operates. People say that we live in a changing world.
People say that Hong Kong changes faster than anywhere
else. I think this has certainly been true in the last ten years.
First and foremost, the conclusion of the Sino-British Joint
Declaration marked the beginning of a twelve-year period of
transition, and has given China, which has always been a
crucial factor in Hong Kong's existence and well-being, even

greater importance and prominence. The Joint Declaration, in a way, has given the People's Republic of China a formal and legal *locus standi* on Hong Kong affairs via the Sino-British Joint Liaison Group, the Land Commission, and other consultative channels. As 1997 approaches, China is seeking to have a say—quite often perhaps even a power of veto—over the way Hong Kong is run, particularly when it comes to policies or measures with a continuing effect after 1997.

Because of this—somewhat ironically perhaps—the British involvement also seems to have increased over the last ten years. Whitehall has been exercising more control over the formulation of policies affecting Hong Kong—policies which have traditionally been within Hong Kong's autonomy to determine. This is, I believe, largely due to China's doctrinal refusal to recognize the Hong Kong government, which they still insist on referring to as the 'British Hong Kong government'. They do not wish to see a stool with three legs, even if a three-legged stool is more stable than a two-legged one. They do not want to deal with Hong Kong, which they regard as the third leg, and insist on dealing with Britain. I think it is because of this that the British government has, whether by choice or by force of circumstances, been playing a more direct role, involving itself more in Hong Kong affairs than before the signature of the Joint Declaration.

Perhaps even more significant are the twin factors of the economic restructuring of Hong Kong and the increasing economic integration between Hong Kong and China. With China's adoption of the 'open-door' policy towards the end of the 1970s, and its embarkation on the 'four modernizations' programme, vast new opportunities were opened up in China for Hong Kong business people, particularly the manufacturing sector. At the same time, with the abolition of the 'touch-base' immigration policy in Hong Kong,[7] and the consequent, very sharp decline in the rate of growth of Hong Kong's population and labour force, the cost of doing

[7] Up until October 1980 people who had entered Hong Kong illegally from China were allowed to remain in Hong Kong for settlement if they managed to reach the urban area. This was generally referred to as the 'touch-base' policy. It was abolished in October 1980 since when all illegal immigrants from China have been returned to the Mainland as soon as, and regardless of where, they were apprehended.

business in Hong Kong increased to such an extent that the sort of labour-intensive manufacturing, in which Hong Kong had traditionally excelled, became non-viable.

The consequence of the combination of these two factors —the opening up of China, with the very much greater supply of land and labour at very much cheaper rates, and the cost-push factor in Hong Kong itself—was a phenomenal relocation of Hong Kong's manufacturing base to Southern China. Today, Hong Kong's traditional, light manufacturing base has all but completely moved across the border. Those few manufacturing industries that are still in Hong Kong have remained here not out of choice, but by force of circumstances, as a result of quota controls and origin rules.[8] But where there is a choice, manufacturing has gone to China, and Hong Kong itself has been transforming (or, perhaps more correctly, re-transforming) itself into its traditional role of the entrepôt for China, as well as developing into the management and marketing base, and services centre for the industrial operations inside China.

As a result, the balance of economic and commercial power between the two has changed significantly. Traditionally, China is thought to depend a great deal on Hong Kong for her foreign exchange earnings, and to value it considerably. This is, of course, still true to a large extent. Today, however, one would have reason to think that Hong Kong probably depends more on China than the other way around. To put it another way, the farmer may need the goose's golden eggs, but the goose cannot go on living without the farmer's feed stuffs.

This process of economic integration has naturally led to a sharp increase in contact between the people of Hong Kong and the people of China. Many old barriers are being broken down, but new problems have also appeared. People in Hong Kong are generally encouraged by much of what they see in China. They like the ways in which things are changing for the better—standards of living are improving and policies are heading in the right direction—but they are also

---

[8] The prime example of this is the textiles and clothing industry whose exports to the USA, Europe, and other markets are subject to quantitative restraint under the Arrangement Regarding International Trade in Textiles (commonly known as the 'Multi-fibre Arrangement').

very worried by some aspects of Chinese life, such as red tape, rampant corruption, and the treatment of political dissidents. As a result, differences in the Hong Kong community's attitudes towards China have intensified—particularly between business people and the proverbial man in the street.

But the most significant change in the operating environment of the civil service, and the one which has had the greatest practical impact, has been the introduction in the mid-1980s of elections, and consequently party politics, into the Hong Kong Legislative Council. Of course, we are still in the relatively early days of a process which has taken hundreds of years to evolve in other countries, and the system of party politics in Hong Kong is still in its infancy. It is also an incomplete system, and therefore a rather strange one, in which there is no government party in the legislature and the entire Legislative Council is made up of the opposition.[9] Fortunately in a way, it is not made up of one opposition, but a collection of different groups which often spend as much time and energy opposing each other as they do opposing the government.

Finally, there have been several major changes in the wider international scene which inevitably have had an impact on Hong Kong. The political upheavals in Eastern Europe, and the fall of communism in the former USSR have changed the world's geo-political scene in ways which few people could have foreseen ten years ago. Then, in China itself, the most significant event of the last ten years (apart from the 'open-door' policy) was the Tiananmen Square incident on 4 June 1989. That event has had an immeasurable impact on how people see and assess China, both in Hong Kong and elsewhere. I believe it has also brought about changes in the British government's policies and strategies in its dealings with China. To cite an example—and I think those who know the history of British immigration will know how crucial an element this is in British policy—I believe that, had

---

[9] As of January 1994, the Hong Kong Legislative Council consisted of sixty members, of whom three were civil servants, eighteen were non-civil servants appointed by the Governor (but not obliged to support the government), eighteen were directly elected from geographical constituencies, and twenty-one were indirectly elected from functional constituencies (e.g. trade, industry, labour, teaching).

it not been for the June Fourth Incident, the British Nationality Selection Scheme would simply not have been possible.[10] Hong Kong people had been fighting in vain for decades for freer entry into the United Kingdom. But the June Fourth Incident made the difference and brought about a major change in the British government's policy.

Again, had it not been for the events of 4 June 1989, today's Legislative Council, which was elected in 1991, would have included only ten directly elected members—the number decided upon in the 1989 White Paper on Constitutional Development—rather than the eighteen currently installed.[11] In other areas, too, there has been evidence of new thinking, new approaches, and a new, tougher, 'stand up to China' attitude on the part of the British government.

Changes in the *Modus Operandi* of the Civil Service

How have all these changes affected the *modus operandi* of the civil service in Hong Kong? Let us recall, for a moment, the traditional picture that I painted earlier of a Hong Kong run by a professional, élite, apolitical, impartial, reasonably open-minded, career civil service. It was a Hong Kong which had no democracy in name or form, but which enjoyed full civil rights and liberties, as well as the rule of law—a very strong safeguard against the misuse of power by civil

[10] The British Nationality Selection Scheme was announced in October 1990. Under the Scheme, the Governor of Hong Kong could recommend to the Secretary of State up to 50,000 heads of households in Hong Kong to be registered as British citizens, i.e. they would be granted the right of abode in the United Kingdom, without having to settle there for any period of time.

[11] In the 1988 White Paper, which was published after extensive public consultation, the Hong Kong government announced that it had decided to postpone the introduction of directly elected members to the Legislative Council until 1991, rather than 1988 as originally suggested. The White Paper recommended the introduction of ten directly elected members in 1991. The events of 4 June 1989 resulted in renewed pressure from some sectors of the community for a faster pace in the move towards democratic elections. Following discussions with the Chinese government in late 1989 and early 1990, the Foreign and Commonwealth Secretary confirmed to the British Parliament in February 1990 that the Hong Kong Legislative Council would have eighteen directly elected seats in 1991.

servants. It was a Hong Kong in which, through the system of appointments and cross-memberships between various bodies, intricate relationships were established between the executive—made up of the civil service and its non-civil service advisers—and the legislature; and these relationships provided a reasonable assurance of legislative support for the executive's policies and decisions.[12]

The introduction of elections and party politics into the Legislative Council has brought about fundamental changes in the traditional relationship between the executive and the legislature. Indeed it has resulted in a complete severance of that relationship—a complete separation of the executive and the legislature. There are now only three people who are common members of the Executive Council and the Legislative Council, and all three are civil servants: the Chief Secretary, the Financial Secretary, and the Attorney General. And from 1995 onwards, even those three will have left the Legislative Council, and there will probably be no common membership at all between the two councils. Thus, the executive can no longer count on receiving the support of the legislature for the legislation it needs, or the financial provision that the legislature has the power to vote. Civil servants increasingly have to engage in persuasion, in lobbying, and also, in the style of the new Patten administration, in going directly to the people. They have to undertake more accounting in public, and face a great deal more controversy.

As a consequence of this, the civil service has inevitably lost some of the initiative and control that it was once able to exercise. Today Branch Secretaries can no longer take complete control of their own agenda and priorities. They cannot even control their own diaries as much as they would like to. Their political role has become much more prominent, and much more time and energy has to be devoted to political activities. Let me illustrate this with some statistics. Within the ten-year period between 1982/3 and 1992/3, the

---

[12] Typically, some members of the Legislative Council were appointed to serve concurrently as members of the Executive Council or as chairmen of key advisory boards and committees. Because they were directly and personally involved in the formulation of government policies, they could be expected to support those policies in the Legislative Council, and to try and carry their Legislative Council colleagues along with them.

number of Legislative Council sittings nearly doubled from
twenty-two to forty-two, and the average length of each sitting also more than doubled from two to five hours. Thus,
the amount of time that many senior civil servants had to
spend at sittings of the Legislative Council increased four-
fold.[13] The number of questions that they had to answer—
i.e. the number of main or original questions which were
notified in advance—more than trebled from 194 to 612. The
number of supplementary questions—i.e. impromptu follow-
up questions seeking further elucidation of the replies to the
main questions—also rose from just over 300 to 868. And
the number of motion debates initiated by members who
were not civil servants rose from two during 1982/3 to 62
during 1992/3.

Of course, attendance at the formal sittings of the Legislative
Council is not the only political activity that senior civil servants have to undertake. There are numerous panels, bills
committees, and other standing or *ad hoc* committees of the
Legislative Council, and civil servants are usually required to
attend meetings of these bodies whenever issues relevant to
their own responsibilities are discussed. According to my own
experience over the past ten years—during 1982/3, I was not
yet a Branch Secretary, but I was working very closely with
one—the average time that a Branch Secretary had to spend
dealing with the Legislative Council, and with issues initiated by the Council, certainly multiplied by more than ten.
But despite the huge increase in workload between 1983
and 1993, the number of Branch Secretaries has remained
unchanged at sixteen. The total size of the civil service has
not grown very much either. Over this same ten-year period, the total strength of the civil service grew by a total of
9 per cent, or an average of 0.8 per cent a year. I suppose
one can conclude from these statistics that civil service productivity has increased very considerably.

All in all, today's civil servants do much more in the way
of selling and defending policies and have relatively less control over their initiation and formulation. Coupled with the

---

[13] Branch Secretaries are not members of the Legislative Council, but attend
its sittings in order to move government bills, answer questions from members, and take part in debates.

approach of 1997 and the recent deterioration in Sino-British relations, this has resulted in the Hong Kong government's policies becoming more short-term. The fact is that many of the longer term issues require consultation with China, but nowadays the two sides seem unable to reach agreement on anything.

Problems and Challenges facing the Civil Service

This sort of situation naturally presents a very great challenge to the civil service. How has the civil service coped? I have to say, and I can do so without blushing now, that I think it has coped extremely well. I think Hong Kong's civil service, despite the very difficult circumstances in which it has to operate, remains one of the most dedicated and hard-working civil services in the world, and one of the cleanest and most efficient. Furthermore, whilst major changes in the operating environment have inevitably brought about changes in the *modus operandi* of the civil service, in practice the government is still executive-led, and the civil service still has a crucial role to play, despite appearances and perceptions to the contrary. The crux of the matter is that, although the government may be called upon more often to account to the legislature and to the public at large, it cannot be voted out of power. This underlying strength gives the civil service the authority that they need to do their job properly.

Nevertheless, there has been some visible erosion of the quality of performance of the civil service in terms of administrative efficiency and of the speed and certainty of decision-making. Life is becoming more difficult and uncomfortable for the more senior civil servants, not only because of the trials and pressures of their present work, but also, and I think far more significantly, because of the uncertainties over their own future after 1997.

These uncertainties should not and need not have arisen. The Joint Declaration and the Basic Law have made it very clear that Hong Kong civil servants may all remain in employment and continue their service after 1997, with pay, allowances, benefits, and conditions of service no less favourable than before. The exception is that Chinese nationals only may occupy the posts of principal officials (equivalent to the present Branch Secretaries and above). Given the provisions of the Joint Declaration and the Basic Law for the maintenance of Hong Kong's systems and lifestyle, and a smooth transfer of government, it would obviously make sense to have a civil service 'through train' across 1997. I firmly believe that most civil servants, particularly those in the senior ranks, remain dedicated and committed to Hong Kong, and are well prepared and able to ride that 'through train' and continue to contribute to the good government of Hong Kong. I also believe, equally firmly, that the Chinese side fully recognizes the importance of the civil service in Hong Kong. Unfortunately, the lack of trust and cooperation between Britain and China, caused largely, it appears, by disagreement over the future political structure and electoral arrangements, is making it very difficult indeed to see how the continuity of the civil service is to be assured.

The British approach seems to be to try and put in place a system that works so well that the Chinese side would not wish to change it. The Chinese, on the other hand, have already made it clear, almost as a matter of principle, that they will not accept the wholesale inheritance of what the British will be leaving behind. They have now established bodies to draw up plans for the re-election of the Legislative Council, the Municipal Councils, and the District Boards in 1997, as well as for the post-1997 political structure. So far, however, it is still very unclear what those plans are going to comprise, or whether they will work and be supported, or at least accepted, by the people of Hong Kong. It is also very unclear whether the individual civil servants, who will be occupying the most senior posts in the Hong Kong government in June 1997, will be able to continue to work in equivalent posts in the government of the Hong Kong Special Administration Region (SAR). Some of them have been publicly criticized by the Chinese for various actions or comments they have made the performance of their present duties.

As a result, civil servants, particularly local senior civil servants, are in a very difficult position. On the one hand, it would make sense to establish good working relations with the future sovereign power, in order to gain its confidence and trust in their ability to exercise the autonomy that has been promised in the Joint Declaration to the future Hong Kong SAR. On the other hand, their professional ethics require them to work within the boundaries of the 'corporate objectives' of the existing Hong Kong government. Most of them rationalize their position by insisting that they are working in the best interests of Hong Kong, and I do not doubt that for a moment. Unfortunately, sharply divided views within the community often make it difficult to judge what is best for Hong Kong, what the people of Hong Kong really want.

In the absence of Sino-British cooperation to ensure a smooth transition, what attitude should a civil servant take? When the British government, the Chinese government, and different sectors of the Hong Kong community are all pulling in different directions, what can be the right decision for him or her to make? These questions are not at all easy to answer, and different individuals have different views and responses.

But one thing is clear: we do have a very good civil service, one we can be proud of and thankful for. It would be absolute nonsense to lose the continuity that only it can provide. For the sake of Hong Kong and its continued success, Britain and China really must put their differences aside, and reassure and harness the civil service. Meanwhile, I suggest that the best civil servants can do is to maintain their professional integrity and do the job as best they can. They should concentrate their energy on practical issues concerning the economic and social well-being of the people of Hong Kong. I believe that politics and elections are but means to an end, and there can be a variety of means to the same end. I also believe that there is much more to life than politics and elections. In the final analysis, it is the welfare of the community that counts, and it is the welfare of the community that the civil service should work for.

3   The Changing Role of the Common Law

HENRY LITTON

THERE ARE few legal problems which do not require the application of first principles. In some respects a judge is like a mechanic. You may have the most complex and sophisticated machine sitting in the garage awaiting the attentions of the mechanic: he would be a fool to go in there without a screwdriver and a spanner. So it is with the Law.

The theme of my talk is the changing role of the common law. I was nudged in this direction by a number of cases decided recently in the courts, particularly in the United Kingdom, indicating that a new philosophy is afoot, a new impatience with out-moded practices is astir. In relation to civil cases, nowhere is this better than in Bingham M. R.'s judgement in the *Arab Monetary Fund* case where he said:

> The judge has to try to press the hearing firmly . . . to a conclusion, conscious that one man's six months in court might be the next man's denial of justice. Judges are constantly being urged to be robust and interventionist to mitigate the blemish on the legal system which protracted trials, civil as well as criminal, have become. . . . [Judges] are not to fear that their professional conduct would be impugned because management decisions, taken one-by-one, with reasons given and no eye on the scoreboard of the parties' respective successes and failures to date, were felt by one party to be unreasonably favourable to the other.

Judiciaries all over the common-law world are examining new concepts of positive case management. A quiet revolution is afoot and soon, I perceive, it will be regarded as the duty of a trial judge to ensure that cases are disposed of expeditiously and economically. Justice is, by definition, thrown out of the window if there is inordinate delay, and the legal costs mount up. Lord Denning, in a sense, represented the old school. He was forever pushing the frontiers of liability in negligence, and seeking to dissolve the sanctity of contracts. He was inclined to enlarge the categories of relationships giving rise to the duty of care in tort, e.g. *Dutton v. Bognor Regis Urban Council* [1972] 1 QB 373, and to relieve parties from their contractual obligations by introducing the concept of inequality of bargaining power, e.g. *Lloyds Bank v. Bundy* [1975] QB 326.

It is doubtful whether Lord Denning had fully considered the wider implications of these judgements: the fact that, in the one case, he was helping to push up insurance premia, to the detriment of the small man, and in the other he was abetting the increase of legal costs by expanding the scope of mutual discovery. How deep is the other party's pocket? That would have been a proper subject for discovery and interrogatories if Lord Denning had his way. If it was legitimate in the process of litigation to show that old Herbert Bundy was poor, in the case of *Lloyds Bank v. Bundy*, was it also legitimate to demonstrate that Lloyds Bank was rich? If this became a real issue in the litigation, where would mutual discovery end?

Lord Denning was prone to chide the Law Lords as 'timorous spirits' and was, for a couple of generations, the hero of academic lawyers and students. I am not sure that this admiration is shared by practising lawyers and judges. Listen to what Harman L. J. said in *Bridge v. Campbell Discount Co. Ltd* [1962] 2 WLR 596 at 605:

> Equitable principles are, I think, perhaps rather too often bandied about in common law courts as though the Chancellor still had only the length of his own foot to measure when coming to a conclusion. Since the time of Lord Eldon anyhow the system of equity for good or evil has been a very precise one, and equitable jurisdiction is exercised only on well-known principles. There are some who would have it otherwise, and I think Lord Denning is one of them. He, it will be remembered, invented an equity called the equity of the deserted wife. That distressful female's condition has really not been improved at all now that this so-called equity has been analysed.

And in the same case Viscount Simonds said, ' "Unconscionable" must not be taken to be a panacea for adjusting any

contract between competent persons when it shows a rough
edge to one side or the other.'

The courts, in seeing the trend of things, began a retreat
in the 1980s. Thus, we see the Privy Council in *Tai Hing
Cotton v. Liu Chong Hing Bank* [1986] AC 80 abandoning the
broad formulation of the duty of care in *Anns v. Merton
London Borough Council*, holding that a customer owed his
bank no duty of care to prevent fraud by his employees; and,
in *China and South Sea Bank v. Tan Soon-gin, George*, [1990]
1 HKLR 546, the Privy Council reversed the Hong Kong Court
of Appeal, holding that a creditor was under no duty to protect the interests of a guarantor by exercising judgment as
to whether shares held by way of security for its customer's
debts should be sold. There, the respondent Mr Tan, had
argued that if the bank had sold the shares he had pledged
early in the market he would not have been called upon to
pay on his personal guarantee. Those shares were at first
ample security for the debts of a company called Filomena
Ltd; later, the shares became worthless, and the Bank looked
to Mr Tan personally for payment. The Hong Kong Court of
Appeal had held that the tort of negligence was wide enough
to encompass the bank's 'duty of care' to Mr Tan, but the
Privy Council said, 'The tort of negligence has not yet subsumed all torts and does not supplement the principles of
equity or contractual obligations.'

A striking illustration of the court's robust approach is
Wharf Properties v. Cumine [1991] 2 HKLR 154. After the litigation had been on foot for four years, Wharf's statement
of claim against the architects was struck out as an abuse of
the court's process—a jurisdiction which, prior to that case,
was rarely exercised. The fact that, in a major piece of commercial litigation, a professionally drafted statement of claim
could be disposed of in this way came as a surprise to many
lawyers.

These are examples of the court's robust approach. What
I am dealing with here are rather esoteric and technical aspects
of the common law. As I went deeper into the preparation
of my notes for this talk I realized that my aim had been
too ambitious: an explanation of the subtle changes of emphasis in the common law over a decade would have brought
me into too many nooks, crevices, and dark corners.

What I propose to do in this talk is therefore to paint a broad panoramic view of changes in the law as I see it, from the rather dizzy heights of the Court of Appeal.

Criminal Law

The 1980s saw the emergence of the massive and complex commercial fraud trial, of which the Carrian case still stands as a startling example, terminated upon the ruling of the judge (the late Barker, J. A.) after hearings lasting over one year.

Unless there is a radical reform of the system, cases like this, involving thousands of documents and spanning long periods of time, will become almost untriable. As it is, they are only triable in court if there is meticulous preparation by the prosecution beforehand and cooperation by the defence. Who is to say that such cases will not get even more complex, particularly if they involve cross-border elements?

The law does not oblige the defence to cooperate in the preparation of the case for trial, beyond the lawyers' professional duty to assist in the due administration of justice. But where cooperation is not forthcoming it does not necessarily mean that the lawyers are being deliberately obstructive. They may, for instance, have difficulties in obtaining instructions from their clients, or are simply unsure, timid, indecisive, or even downright incompetent. Yet the fact remains that once the basic facts have been analysed, and the transactions traced to their source, there is seldom room for dispute over the main events. Usually, each step in the proceedings is well documented: for instance, the movement of funds from one account to another. This can be illustrated with charts and diagrams which speak for themselves. A robust judge who has thoroughly familiarized himself with the papers—itself no mean task—would order the production of these visual aids.

It was with a view to streamlining the procedures for dealing with such cases that the Complex Commercial Crimes Ordinance was enacted in July 1988. This Ordinance has turned out not to be a great success. The machinery devised for dealing with such cases is, itself, too complex. The Ordinance has not in fact been much used by the Director of Public Prosecutions in recent years.

To achieve real reform, as I see it, two basic steps must be taken. First, there must be a fundamental change in the approach to criminal trials by the presiding judges. Second, the powers of the presiding judges must be enlarged by legislation. Let me elaborate upon these two points.

As to the approach by the presiding judge, his traditional role as the passive umpire is no longer valid. The march of events has swept him by, leaving him blinking in the sunlight. To achieve practical justice and ensure that trials are brought speedily to a conclusion, the judge must now play an active role. He must be prepared to intervene and, if necessary, to reshape the prosecution case by focusing on essential matters. To have the confidence to do this, the judge must be totally on top of the case. This means that he must be given time to prepare, by reading and absorbing the papers beforehand. Accordingly, the present system, whereby judges are expected to render efficient service as a result only of the hours they spend in court, is no longer adequate. Just as the parties' legal advisers must have time for preparation, so must the judge. When I was in practice I used to say to my clients, 'Remember this. A trial is like an iceberg. What you see in court is the tip. Nine-tenths of the effort is in the preparation.'

Occasionally, time alone would not enable the judge to get to grips with the papers. He would need help—a roadmap to steer him through the box files. In such circumstances I see no reason why he should not call for a pre-trial hearing, for the sole purpose of having prosecution counsel to assist him in this respect.

To go on to the second point, the judge must be given the power, if necessary, to declare that certain primary facts are binding upon the parties, for the purposes of the trial, whether they have agreed the facts or not. This will not be an easy jurisdiction to exercise and, as a proposal, it will be regarded by many as heretical; it will be said to undermine the traditional role of the judge as the impartial umpire. But, as the saying goes: 'Talk does not cook rice'. To achieve expeditious practical justice, judges must be empowered to act. At present, under the Complex Commercial Crimes Ordinance, if the judge considers that certain facts should be agreed, and the defence declines to cooperaté, the only sanction the judge can impose is legal costs: to require the defendant to pay the costs incurred in proving those facts. In a case like Carrian, this would be no sanction at all. In my view, the judge should be given real powers. Without such powers, the Complex Commercial Crimes Ordinance will remain ineffective.

Usually, in these complex commercial crime cases, investigation by the Commercial Crimes Bureau of the Police and by the ICAC[1] is meticulous. They would have spent hundreds of man-hours hunting through the documents, engaged in a complex paper-chase. But it is not their function to fashion the material into shape ready for trial. That is the role of the lawyers. It would be a misfortune if, after months of painstaking preparation, the efforts of the investigators were set at naught by the fumblings of the lawyers, or the mistakes of the judge—things that could easily happen if one was not thoroughly at home with the material.

Crime and Punishment

It may be of interest to recall that in the earliest days of the common law, crimes were treated as wrongs for which compensation was made to the victim. Norman French law in the Middle Ages had a concept called *deodand*: forfeiture of a thing of value which was the instrument of crime. The notion of public crimes took a long time to develop. Is it possible that there was considerable wisdom behind the medieval concept and that, one day, we may come full circle?

As we all know, the prisons in Hong Kong are overcrowded and there are no signs of any diminution in the incidence of crime. I am not aware of any statistics on the cost to the community of keeping convicted criminals in prison in Hong Kong. Recent studies in the United Kingdom have shown that, on average, it costs £430 a week (about HK$5,160) to keep someone in prison. In a speech given to the New Assembly of Churches in the United Kingdom in October 1993, Lord Woolf said:

> Just pause for a moment and speculate what some victims of crime could do with £22,000 a year or there-

---

[1] The Independent Commission Against Corruption.

abouts, which is the cost of keeping his or her assailant locked up in prison. Remember that eventually that prisoner is going to come out of prison, and the question then will be: is he more or less likely to commit a further crime? Bear in mind that the prisoner hopefully has family ties, and that those ties are inevitably going to be damaged by the fact of imprisonment. A broken family may result, with the consequent danger to the children of that family; that prisoner may be creating the situation in which the children will grow up to commit the sins of their parents.[2]

The bill recently introduced in the Legislative Council, the Post-Release Supervision of Prisoners Bill, seems to me a move in the right direction. The Bill provides for the release under supervision of certain categories of prisoners on the order of a board. The success of the scheme will depend upon two key elements: (i) the way the board functions and (ii) the quality of the supervision.

The first causes concern. The board will consist of unpaid volunteers appointed by the Governor, senior people in the community squeezing time from their busy schedules for such voluntary work. Is this adequate for the purpose? If the board is to be more than a rubber-stamp, it would have to read and absorb a great deal of material on each case, and consider the opinions of psychiatrists and social workers. Who would have time for that, on a voluntary basis?

I must confess that, the more I sit as a judge, dealing with criminal appeals, the more I wonder how it is possible for a young man of average (or perhaps below average) ability, growing up in a resettlement estate where his parents are at work all day, or perhaps from a broken home, subject to peer pressure, assailed by television and video films showing violence, discourtesy, defiance of authority on a daily basis—I wonder how it is possible that such a young man could grow up to be a decent, caring, self-respecting, law-abiding citizen. He finds little moral guidance from organized society, so he seeks his own identity in the mob, the gangs in the playgrounds and the streets. Eventually he comes before us and we punish him for being a member of a triad society or for

---

[2] *The Times*, 12 October 1993. Lord Woolf is a well-known Law Lord.

other similar crimes. Sometimes I wonder, are we punishing the victim or the criminal?

There have, in recent years, been moves to liberalize the criminal law. In July 1991 the Crimes (Amendment) Ordinance was passed to decriminalize homosexual acts between consenting adults in private. This followed intensive debate in the community over a long period: when the bill was first introduced in July 1990, there was vociferous opposition to it. Some members of the Legislative Council suggested that this was creeping Western decadence. I am not aware, since the law on homosexuality was amended two and a half years ago, that society has become more decadent. If it has become more corrupt since then, I am not aware that homosexuals are in anyway responsible. The question I ask is this: have the real problems of society been addressed? Or are these cosmetic changes?

At about the same time two further changes to the criminal law were made. One was to abolish corporal punishment and the other to remove the death sentence from the statute book. These were *nominal* changes because both forms of punishment had become, in effect, obsolete long before their repeal.

These are, I suggest, barely scratches on the surface of society, and they leave the fundamental questions of crime and punishment untouched.

Permanent Stay of Criminal Proceedings

Until fairly recently, the criminal process was seen as something slow, structured, and inexorable. It is not possible to prosecute for every crime committed and to pursue every criminal. But, once a prosecution is launched, it must result in either an acquittal or the conviction of the defendant. In this way, the majesty of the law is upheld and respect for the law maintained.

There has, however, at common law always been a remedy, hardly ever employed, to stay a criminal process permanently because of delay; where the delay in a prosecution has been such that the defendant has suffered real prejudice, no fair trial could then result. On the other hand, the law imposes no limitation period on serious crimes. Some crimes require more time to investigate than others. The effluxion of time alone, therefore, could hardly ever provide the ground for a stay of criminal proceedings.

The enactment of the Hong Kong Bill of Rights has given fresh impetus to challenges to the criminal process through delay. Article 5(3) of the Bill of Rights provides that, 'Anyone arrested or detained on a criminal charge . . . shall be entitled to trial within a reasonable time or to release.' Article 11(2)(c) provides a minimum guarantee to persons accused of crime, 'to be tried without undue delay'. In the case of *A.G. v. Charles Cheung Wai Bun* (1993) 1 HKCLR 249, the defendant successfully invoked the provisions of the Hong Kong Bill of Rights and obtained a stay of the charge of conspiracy to defraud a bank. There, the underlying facts were highly complex and went back some ten years. The defendant successfully demonstrated that the delay (which was partly self-induced) had caused him real prejudice. The matter was eventually considered by the Privy Council. Lord Woolf stated the law in these terms:

> Naturally, the longer the delay the more likely it will be that the prosecution is at fault, and that the delay has caused prejudice to the defendant; and the less that the prosecution has to offer by explanation, the more easily can fault be inferred. But the establishment of these facts is only one step on the way to a consideration of whether, in all the circumstances, the situation created by the delay is such as to make it an unfair employment of the powers of the court any longer to hold the defendant to account.

Since this case, resort to the remedy of a stay of criminal proceedings has greatly increased. Unless this jurisdiction is exercised with robust common sense, it may become a self-fulfilling process: the proceedings to stay, based on alleged delay, may themselves inordinately delay the trial. If this were to happen it would indeed bring the law into disrepute.

A difficult balance must be struck. Where allegations of serious delay, which on their face are not frivolous, are made, they must be properly investigated. They may involve disputed evidence, as occurred in the case of *The Queen v. Deacon*

Chiu Cr. App. 122/92, 20 April 1993 (unreported).[3] But should this process take months and months of the court's time? There is, in my view, great danger in over-sophistication in our system. In an attempt to do perfect justice, the courts can lose sight of their main function, that of practical justice. The search for ideal justice, as was once said, is the last infirmity of a noble mind.

Hong Kong's Bill of Rights

The Bill of Rights came into effect on 8 June 1991. Any law which is inconsistent with the provisions of the Bill of Rights is, by the operation of Section 3(2) of the Ordinance, repealed as of that date.

The Bill of Rights has generated an enormous volume of litigation. Despite the frequency with which its provisions are invoked, there have been few instances of existing laws being held to be violations of the Bill of Rights. In those instances where the Bill has been successfully invoked, the court could say that the legislature had plainly gone too far in its encroachment upon fundamental freedoms—as in the leading case of *The Queen v. Sin Yau Ming* (1992) 1 HKCLR 127, which dealt with some of the evidential presumptions which existed in the Dangerous Drugs Ordinance. As the law then stood, possession of a mere 0.5 grammes or five packets of cannabis would have given rise to a presumption of possession for the purpose of unlawful trafficking. It is not surprising that such a statutory provision should have been struck down as being inconsistent with the presumption of innocence in Article 11(1) of the Bill of Rights.

Closer to the borderline is the case of *The Queen v. Lau Shiu-wah* [1992] HKDCLR 11 where the District Court held that Section 29(6)(a)(1) of the Theft Ordinance was also inconsistent with Article 11(1) and therefore deemed repealed. That section of the Theft Ordinance says that anyone who obtains property by means of a cheque which is refused payment shall, until the contrary is proved, be deemed to have obtained the property knowing that such cheque would not be honoured.

---

[3] In this case the accused person again complained of inordinate delay by the prosecution.

Normally a person who delivers a cheque in payment for property would know whether the cheque is likely to be honoured or not. There seems nothing irrational or disproportionate in saying that, given the normal experience of mankind, a presumption of knowledge should arise. On the evidence in the *Lau Shiu-wah* case, the court held that it did arise, so the prosecution did not in fact have to rely on the statutory presumption. The District Judge ruled nevertheless that this section in the Theft Ordinance should, from 8 June 1991, be repealed.

The jurisprudence in this area of the law in Hong Kong is still in its infancy. Its impact has already been substantial. For instance, the enactment of the Drug Trafficking (Recovery of Proceeds) Ordinance was held up for a considerable time because it was feared that its provisions might conflict with the Bill of Rights. Then, in *A.G. v. Lo Chakman* [1993]3 WLR 329, Mr Justice Gall held that Section 25(l) and (4) of that Ordinance were inconsistent with the presumption of innocence; they were hence repealed. It took nearly eighteen months for that decision to be reversed in the Privy Council; meanwhile banks in Hong Kong refused to cooperate with the police and withheld information concerning the movement of funds of suspected drug traffickers. For a time, Hong Kong became an important centre for laundering drug money.

It can be said, however, that the 'honeymoon period' between lawyers and the Bill of Rights is over. Possibly, its effect may not be as profound as was thought by some academic lawyers when it was first enacted. With its arcane vocabulary and amorphous concepts imported wholesale from international law, it was thought at one time that the Bill had brought a whole new 'human rights culture' into the Hong Kong courts. This may be overstating the position. In *Attorney General v. Charles Cheung Wai Bun* the Privy Council said that the provisions of Article II (2)(c) (right to trial without 'undue delay') and Article 10 (right to a 'fair hearing') added nothing to the common law 'abuse of process' principles, which could just as viably have protected the defendant from the abuse of which he complained.

The important point to bear in mind is this: the courts are not, through the Bill of Rights, introducing alien human rights concepts into Hong Kong by the back-door. The courts are simply giving effect to the words of a Hong Kong statute—bearing in mind, of course, in construing the statute, that it is taken from an international treaty, and the words used must be given a broad and liberal interpretation. Arguably, the 'freedoms' guaranteed under the Bill of Rights are essentially the same freedoms as those protected by common law remedies against the exercise of arbitrary government powers.

The Language of the Law

Statute law has, until recently, been enacted only in the English language. The amendment of the Hong Kong Royal Instructions and the enactment of the Official Languages (Amendment) Ordinance 1987 paved the way for the implementation of bilingual laws in Hong Kong.

As from 1987 all new legislation has been enacted in both official languages—English and Chinese. For existing legislation, the Law Drafting Division of the Attorney General's Chambers has been translating the laws into Chinese, for approval by the Bilingual Laws Advisory Committee. This is a massive task. The Advisory Committee has, quite sensibly, decided to give priority to those ordinances most frequently used in the courts or which are likely to be of use to large sections of the public. At the last count, the Chinese text of only eleven ordinances out of a total of over 500 have been declared authentic.

The aim of the government to make the law more accessible to the people of Hong Kong is commendable. This leads me to the question of the use of language in court proceedings. Section 5(2) of the Official Languages Ordinance requires proceedings in all the courts, apart from Magistrates courts and some statutory tribunals, to be conducted in the English language. The presiding judge has no discretion in the matter. This appears to be in conflict with Article 9 of the Basic Law which declares that Chinese and English may be used. It is plain therefore that Section 5(2) of the Official Languages Ordinance must be amended to avoid that conflict.

It is the primary duty of the presiding judge—whatever the court—to conduct the proceedings in such a way as to best facilitate the resolution of the issues before him, for the attainment of justice. Where a party has engaged lawyers to represent him in court, the choice of language is that of the lawyers and that choice will invariably be English. But if a party appears before a court in person, using a language other than English, that party must also be heard. Thus, an efficient translation service must be regarded as a normal function of the court in a multi-racial community such as ours, irrespective of the 1997 change of sovereignty.

Assume, for example, that a party acting in person presents a legal document in, say, Vietnamese—what should the court do? Under the present law, the registry will refuse to receive it, forcing the litigant, in effect, to undergo the expense himself of having it translated into English. Assume the document to be in Chinese—should the court act in the same way? As Section 5(2) of the Official Languages Ordinance stands at present, this document would also be rejected. As I read Article 9 of the Basic Law, such rejection would, after 30 June 1997, be unlawful.

It seems to me that there is now an overwhelming case for urgently improving the translation services offered by the courts at all levels, so that documents received in Chinese can be translated into English and, when necessary, documents in English can be translated into Chinese. This is a service for which the public will simply have to pay, if the system is to operate after 1997. The only alternative, as I see it, is for Legal Aid to be given in every instance, irrespective of merit or indeed whether the litigants desire legal representation or not. This may turn out to be a far more expensive option than the establishing of translation services in the courts.

It can even be argued that the system as exists at present is, inherently, unfair. Take the instance of a criminal trial in the District Court. The charge, in English, is read to the accused in Chinese but he is not provided with a Chinese translation of the written document. If he is convicted, the Reasons for Verdict and Sentence are, of course, translated to him in Chinese in open court but, again, no Chinese text of the document is given to him. Acting in person, he would find it very difficult to exercise his right of appeal, since he would have nothing in his hands which he could actually read. Friends and relatives sitting in court, if they do not speak English, would find it hard to know the Reasons for Verdict and Sentence, since the interpreter's job is not to make his interpretation audible to everyone in court.

The raw fact of the matter is that whilst we profess in Hong Kong to have a sophisticated legal system, the instruments by which it is carried out are crude. It is odd that for relatively minor meetings of, say, subcommittees of the New Airport Consultative Committee, a simultaneous translation service is provided by the government; yet, for a major trial, of the utmost public importance, the courts are simply not equipped to render such a service.

In some respects it can be said that the Judiciary is operating a computer-age system with Stone-Age tools.

4 A Challenging Decade for the Business Community: A Productivity Perspective

GEORGE SHEN

ABOUT FIFTEEN years ago, China began to launch drastic economic reforms. The impact was first felt in the agricultural sector when farmers were given permission to sell their products on the free market after meeting state purchase quotas. In the meantime, China also decided to open its doors to the outside world, and steps were taken to establish Special Economic Zones (SEZs) in the coastal provinces—notably Shenzhen and Zhuhai in Guangdong—with a view to attracting foreign investment. By 1984, agricultural reforms had met with such success that it was decided to expand the scope of reform to the industrial sector in the urban areas. By that time, considerable foreign capital had poured into the SEZs, mainly from Hong Kong. 1984 was also a year when economic and political events significant to Hong Kong took place. Economically, it was the year in which the advanced countries of the world had fully recovered from the recession of the early 1980s, and were heading towards one of the longest boom periods in the post-war era; politically, the year saw China and Britain reach accord on the future of Hong Kong. These events helped usher in one of Hong Kong's most prosperous decades.

Almost ten years have elapsed and many significant changes have taken place since then. According to latest data released by the Census and Statistics Department, Hong Kong's gross domestic product (GDP)—at 1980 constant prices—has increased from just over HK$170 billion in 1984 to HK$287.4 billion in 1992. Per capita income, also at constant 1980 prices, has risen from HK$33,205 in 1984 to HK$49,453 in 1992 (in current prices, per capita GDP in 1992 was HK$127,778 or about US$16,380). Hong Kong's business community can today look back with a sense of pride at the achievements of the past decade. Merchandise exports increased from US$28.3 billion in 1984 to US$119.5 billion in 1992. The Hang Seng Index, considered the barometer of Hong Kong's economy, was 871.06 points on the first trading day in 1984, but closed at 12,086.49 points on the first trading day in 1994 (Fig. 4.1). In 1984, Hong Kong was already a regional financial centre, but today it has become the focus of attention for the developed and developing countries alike. This is because Hong Kong is not only the springboard to China—a burgeoning economy and a vast market for both capital and consumer goods—but also a model free-market economy with considerable influence over China's economic reform. According to the latest edition of the *International Financial Yearbook* issued by the International Monetary Fund, foreign direct investment in China increased from US$386 million in 1982 (when figures first became available) to US$3,453 million in 1992, and it is now common knowledge that more than two thirds of such investments originated from or were channelled through Hong Kong.

Why has Hong Kong's business flourished since 1984? I think the most important contributing factor lies in one word: change. Apart from the changes in GDP, per capita income, volume of trade, and the Hang Seng Index, many other significant changes, have taken place during the past ten years. It is change that brings dynamism, provides opportunities, offers challenges, and fosters improvement. Of course, change alone does not bring business, wealth, or prosperity. It is the business community's ability to adapt to and take advantage of the developments, or, rather, the willingness to take risks during such transformations, that has been the driving force behind Hong Kong's success.

Businessmen take advantage of developments, and these in turn provide new opportunities for the business community. It is therefore a cycle of change-adaptation-risk-opportunity-challenge which has instilled vitality and energy into the Territory to make Hong Kong what it is today.

Thus we have witnessed transformations in Hong Kong's economic structure, manifested by the decline in the manufacturing sector's share, both in terms of GDP and employed labour force, and the relative increase in the shares of service industries, such as trade, transport, communication,

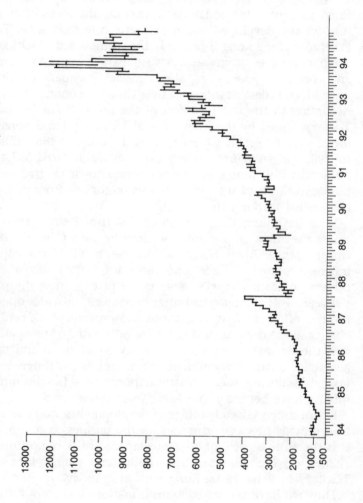

Figure 4.1 Heng Sang Index (January 1984–January 1994)

financing, insurance, real estate, and other areas. We have also witnessed developments in Hong Kong's trade pattern, especially in terms of re-exports *vis-à-vis* China. These transitions did not occur by themselves. They were brought about by changing circumstances, both domestic and international, and by Hong Kong's response to them. It may be said that behind each of these developments, the driving force has been the collective wisdom of the people of Hong Kong, including management and labour, in both the private and public sectors.

These changes are almost common knowledge today, and, hence, I see no need to delve into details here. However, there is one aspect of the transformation which has hitherto been neglected, and which I would like to bring to your notice by sharing with you the findings of my own studies. By this I mean productivity changes.

Productivity Changes

GDP and per capita income growth rates are the most commonly used economic indicators. However, these figures are often deceptive for several reasons. First, a country may register growth in GDP year after year, but still remain poor or without relative improvement in standards of living. This is because while production output may be on the increase, resources are not being utilized efficiently or, more precisely, because resource inputs such as land, labour, capital, and energy are growing at relatively higher rates than those of output or goods and services produced. For the same reason, a company may enjoy increases in its business turnover year after year, but may still fail to experience similar increases in profits. In both cases, an analysis of the situation from a productivity angle will reveal a truer picture, and thus enable solutions to be found to hitherto neglected problems.

It may be pertinent before proceeding further, to give a brief definition of productivity. Productivity is generally defined as the ratio of the output, or collection of goods or services, to the input of one or more of the factors producing it. The change of productivity over time is a useful indicator of whether or not resources are being efficiently used to achieve maximum results, both at the macro and micro levels. However, merely understanding a nation's or a company's productivity, though helpful, is not enough. It is necessary to compare them with those of other nations or companies to find out 'where we stand'. The common methodology accepted internationally today is to look at labour productivity, by using labour (either in terms of number of persons employed or hours worked) as the input measure, and value-added (gross output less the value of intermediate input) as the output measure. The reason for using labour productivity rather than total factor productivity is that labour already reflects the effects of other inputs such as capital, technology, education and training. Also, in developing countries, reliable data on capital input are scarce, thus rendering international comparison difficult.

Hence, for the purpose of this brief talk we will look at Hong Kong's labour productivity at national and sectoral levels and compare them with the other three newly industrializing economies (NIEs) of Asia—namely Korea, Singapore, and Taiwan—and the emerging NIEs of Malaysia and Thailand, all of which are Hong Kong's main competitors.

First let us compare labour productivity growth at the national level (Fig. 4.2). For the period 1981 to 1992 (the year when latest statistical data are available) we will find that the productivity growth rates of Thailand, Hong Kong, Taiwan, and Korea are more or less the same, with Singapore and Malaysia following behind.

It should be noted that the reason that Hong Kong's productivity growth compares favourably with that of the others in Figure 4.2 is because the year 1985 is used as the base year, when Hong Kong's GDP grew only 0.2 per cent and productivity grew at a negative rate of –1.5 per cent. When 1980 is used as the base year, the picture becomes somewhat different (Fig. 4.3). In other words, Hong Kong started at a lower base in 1985 than the other countries. Considering that the productivity levels of Hong Kong and Singapore are about the same, and both are higher than the other NIEs, the similar rates of growth achieved by these NIEs imply that the productivity gap between Hong Kong and its competitors is narrowing. In our ensuing discussion, we should bear this point in mind.

Figure 4.2 Productivity Comparison among NIEs (National Level)

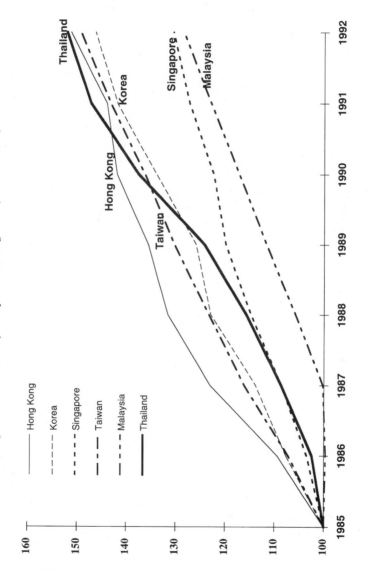

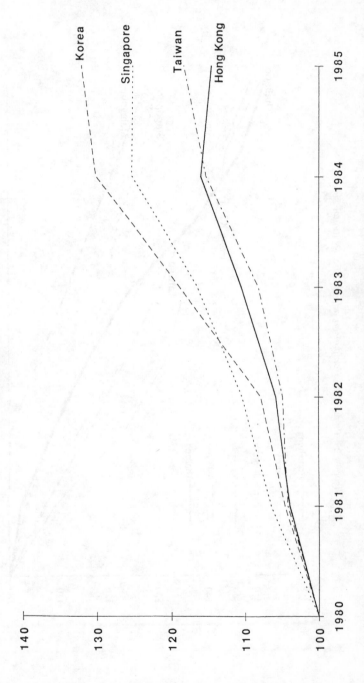

Figure 4.3 Labour Productivity Comparison (National Level)

To get a better picture of Hong Kong's productivity, we need to look further at the various sectors of the economy. However, Hong Kong does not have value-added figures according to economic activities at constant prices, and so far no known attempt has been made to measure productivity at the sectoral level. For the purpose of this paper, I have computed the value-added figures at constant 1985 prices by using a set of different deflators for the various sectors (see Appendix). The sectors I have selected are manufacturing, construction, trade (including wholesale and retail trade, restaurants and hotels), transport and communication (including storage), and finance (including insurance, real estate, and business services). Due to data constraints, comparisons of most sectors are for 1981 to 1990 only, except for the manufacturing sector, which has been estimated until 1992.

The Manufacturing Sector

Let us first look at the manufacturing sector, which is the main pillar of the economy in all NIEs. Here Hong Kong has fared better than all of its competitors except Taiwan (Fig. 4.4). This is understandable because during the period under review, Hong Kong moved most of its labour-intensive manufacturing operations to low labour-cost countries, mainly China, and what remained in Hong Kong consisted merely of operations necessary for certificates of origin purposes, and the more capital-intensive production and managerial functions. Thus, between 1982 and 1992, labour productivity of Hong Kong's manufacturing sector increased, on average, about 7 per cent per annum, a rate higher than most other NIEs.

To Hong Kong, the most important sub-sectors in the manufacturing sector are clothing and textiles (36 per cent of the manufacturing sector's total value-added), fabricated metal and plastic products (over 12 per cent of total value-added), and electronic and electrical products (12.3 per cent of total value-added). Among these, labour productivity growth was the lowest in the clothing and textile industries. The average annual growth during the period was between 5 per cent and 7 per cent per annum. Fabricated-metal and

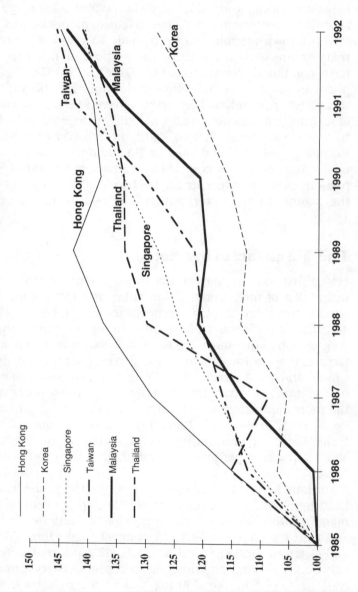

Figure 4.4 Labour Productivity Comparison (Manufacturing Sector)

plastic-products industries had an annual growth rate similar to the whole manufacturing sector—7 per cent. The highest productivity growth, however, was found in the electronic and electrical products industries, which recorded an average annual growth rate of about 10 per cent.

The factors contributing to higher or lower productivity include the percentage of value-added to gross output, the percentage of wages and salaries to value-added, management decision, and competition. The average value-added to gross output of the manufacturing sector during the early 1990s was about 52 per cent, whereas that of the clothing industry was only about 30 per cent, and that of the textile industry around 27 per cent—both well under the industry's average. As to the percentage of wages and salaries to value-added, these two industries were about 72 per cent and 62 per cent respectively—well over the industry's average of 59 per cent. With regard to management decision and competition, the clothing and textile industries were (and still are) sheltered by the quota system, which ensured that they could sell a certain quantity of products every year.[1] The fact that these industries registered a decline in annual productivity growth rates in recent years should be a cause for concern, since the quota system is to be phased out in the coming years, this sub-sector, already a sunset industry, may eventually disappear from Hong Kong.

Construction Sector

Hong Kong's construction sector did not fare very well (Fig. 4.5), showing only about a 14 per cent productivity increase between 1985 and 1990, much lower than that of Thailand, Korea, or Taiwan. One reason for this is the rising cost of construction in Hong Kong, which, apart from Singapore, is the highest in the region.

---

[1] Hong Kong's textile exports to Austria, Canada, the European Community, Finland, Norway, and the United States are governed by bilateral agreements negotiated under the Multi-Fibre Agreement, whereby certain quotas are imposed to limit the growth of such exports. Because Hong Kong started as an exporter of textiles earlier than many other developing economies, it has enjoyed a relatively large export quota under such agreements.

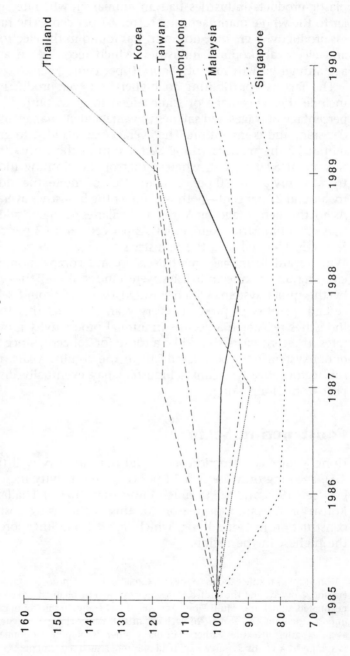

Figure 4.5   Labour Productivity Comparison (Construction Sector)

In recent years, the construction sector has been expecting the PADS programme[2] to come into effect, but delays have put a serious constraint on the industry. With scarcity of land a continuing problem in Hong Kong, public spending on major capital works under increasing scrutiny by the Legislative Council, and inflation causing escalation in construction prices, the need to improve the productivity of the construction sector cannot be overemphasized. Hong Kong may be enjoying a real-estate boom, but the construction sector is certainly in need of greater improvements in productivity and profitability.

Service Sectors

Hong Kong is known as the finance, business, trade, and communications centre of the region, but are we also leaders in productivity in these services? Let us take a look at the labour productivity of the trade, transport, and communications and finance sectors one by one.

On the whole, the rate of productivity growth in the trade sector has been below that of the manufacturing sector. This is because, apart from the wholesale and retail sub-sector, productivity for import/export, which used to have the highest rate of increase in both labour input and value-added output, has shown almost no growth at all. The situation of the restaurants and hotels sub-sectors has been even worse, with labour productivity showing negative rate of growth.

However, Hong Kong still compares favourably with the other NIEs in the trade sector, with only Thailand showing a higher productivity growth rate (Fig. 4.6). But this offers little comfort. Hong Kong has managed to remain a trading centre simply because of its sheer volume of trade compared with other NIEs. Trade volume must be coupled with productivity increase to enable Hong Kong to remain a regional trade centre.

The transport and communications sector attained the highest productivity growth rate, not only within Hong Kong's service industries, but also among other NIEs (Fig. 4.7). This

[2] The Port and Airport Development Strategy (PADS) was unveiled by the Hong Kong government in 1989. It was designed to provide for the growth of both the port and the airport.

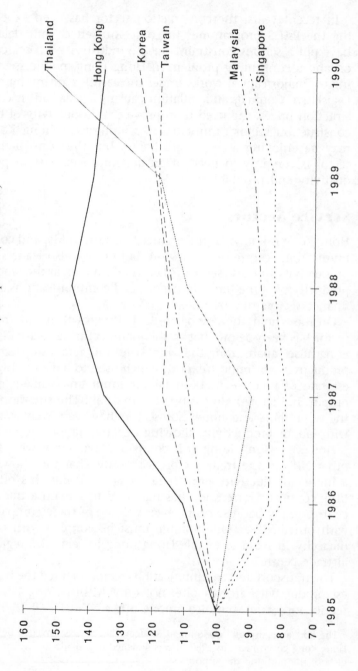

Figure 4.6 Labour Productivity Comparison (Trade Sector)

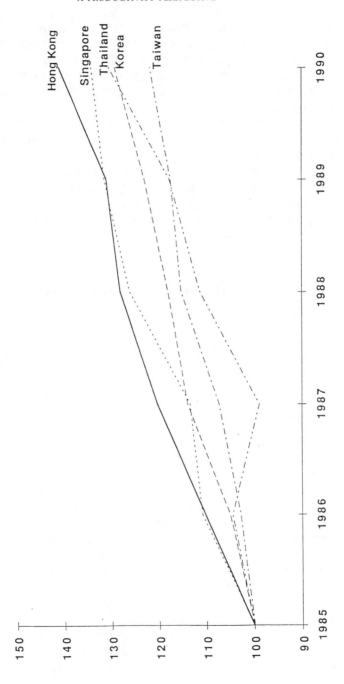

Figure 4.7 Labour Productivity Comparison (Transport & Communications Sector)

is mainly due to technological advancements in communications, contributing to an average annual productivity growth of over 13 per cent during the 1980s. Productivity growth rates of the transport and storage sub-sectors, on the other hand, were well below that of the overall average of the whole economy.

In the finance sector, the finance sub-sector's productivity grew at an average of about 5.6 per cent per annum, whereas insurance, real estate, and business services registered negative growth. This is why the sector as a whole showed negative productivity growth during almost the entire decade of 1980s, rendering Hong Kong's status rather unfavourable compared with the finance sector of the other NIEs. Hong Kong lagged behind Singapore, was about the same as Taiwan, and was only marginally better than Korea (Fig. 4.8).

Comparison amongst Various Sectors

Let us now compare the productivity growth rates of the various sectors with the economy as a whole (Fig. 4.9). We can see that productivity growth rate of the manufacturing sector was higher than the overall average, whereas that of the construction, trade, and finance sectors lagged behind, and that of the transport and communication sectors grew at almost the same rate as the whole economy. This implies that manufacturing is still one of the main pillars of the economy, whereas Hong Kong's position as a service centre is rather dubious, since it is built on volume rather than productivity.

This brings us to the real challenge faced by Hong Kong and its business community. Although we have been able to make Hong Kong into what it is today, we have not been able to restructure our economy successfully. As a result of insufficient productivity improvements in the service sectors, Hong Kong has not yet been transformed from a manufacturing-oriented to a service-oriented economy as a result of lack of sufficient productivity improvement in the service sectors. With manufacturing industries facing stiffer competition, and the tendency to continue to move labour-intensive processes to other locations, Hong Kong's economy will depend more and more on the productivity of the

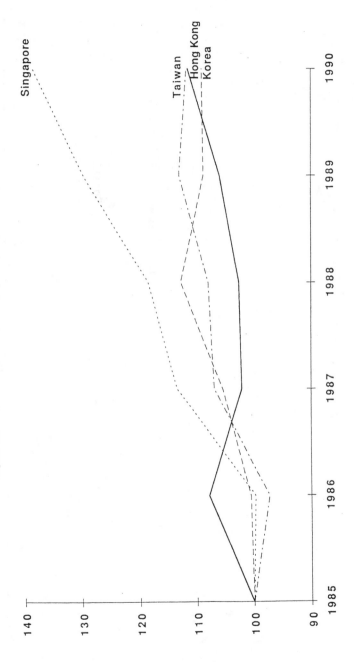

Figure 4.8 Labour Productivity Comparison (Finance Sector)

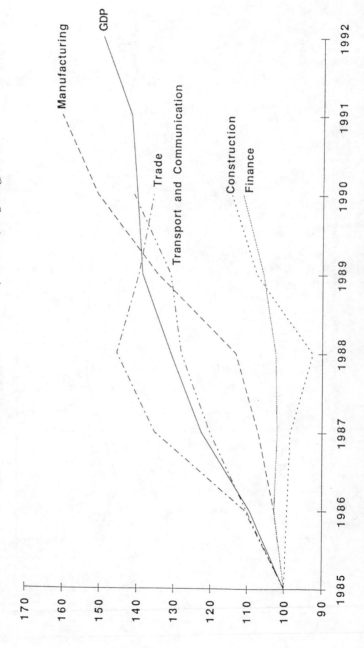

Figure 4.9 Labour Productivity Indexes (Hong Kong)

service sectors, which must be able to compete internationally in terms of cost when offering quality services. Unless we redouble our efforts to raise the productivity of the service sectors—in particular import/export, hotels and restaurants, and insurance and business services—Hong Kong's position as a finance, trade, and communication centre will be at risk.

The China Factor

While on the subject of Hong Kong's economy and its productivity growth, we must take the China factor into account. China has enjoyed a high rate of economic growth for quite some years, and the growth rate of Guangdong province, where the SEZs of Shenzhen and Zhuhai are located, has been even higher. Between 1978 and 1991, China's average annual real growth rate was 8.7 per cent—that of Guangdong, 12.3 per cent. In 1992, China's economy grew by 13 per cent, whereas the growth rate of Guangdong was estimated to be about 25 per cent. The economy was no doubt overheated, and austerity measures were introduced in July 1993.

In terms of productivity, China's labour productivity increased by 88 per cent between 1978 and 1989, the highest amongst Asian economies, while Guangdong's labour productivity increased by 169 per cent during the same period, the highest amongst provinces in China.

It should be remembered, of course, that China's and Guangdong's high productivity increase was due to their low starting point. When we look at productivity level in terms of absolute value-added in constant prices, then China and Guangdong are still far behind any of the NIEs. I have worked out some preliminary figures to compare the productivity levels of China and Guangdong in 1990 with those of the NIEs, by using 100 as the labour productivity level of Hong Kong at 1980 constant prices in US dollars. The outcome is shown in Table 4.1.

When we take the China factor into consideration, common knowledge tells us that Hong Kong's manufacturing industries have not decreased in importance, but have in fact expanded by employing an extra three million workers—

Table 4.1 Comparison of Labour Productivity
Levels, 1990

	Constant Prices US$, 1980
Singapore	103.65
Hong Kong	100.00
Taiwan	62.19
Korea	49.33
Malaysia	38.52
Thailand	12.27
Guangdong	8.83
China	6.79

albeit across the border—producing a lot more than before
production facilities were moved to the SEZs and other parts
of China. Also, the sector's high rate of productivity in Hong
Kong, coupled with an even higher rate of productivity growth
in Hong Kong's joint ventures or wholly-owned operations
in Guangdong, should put Hong Kong in a very favourable
position in terms of international competition. However, we
should not forget that the productivity level of the manufacturing sector in China and Guangdong is less than one-
tenth that of Hong Kong, so that the more Hong Kong
produces in China, the lower the combined average productivity level becomes. In other words, if we took the Hong
Kong-owned manufacturing operations on the other side of
the Shenzhen River as part of the local Hong Kong manufacturing sector, the combined productivity level would become
very low when compared with our competitors. This is certainly not very encouraging, and this is why I think that
moving manufacturing operations into China could be to
Hong Kong's disadvantage.

Moreover, relying heavily on lower factor costs in China
to gain a competitive edge has its drawbacks. Today, Hong
Kong products, whether made locally or in China, are not
only competing with other NIEs, but are in fact competing
with every developing economy in the world, particularly

those in Asia, such as Sri Lanka, Pakistan, and India, to name a few, whose wages are even lower than those in China. Thus, some manufacturers have found that even though their business volume may have increased substantially, their profit has been declining. During the 1970s and early 1980s, it was not uncommon for companies with, say, an annual turnover of HK$500 million, to report profits in the region of 40 per cent of sales. Today, notwithstanding expanded production facilities at reduced unit labour cost in China, profit margins have narrowed considerably. The argument has always been that, without moving into China, profit margins would have dropped even further. Everybody knows that competition through price-cutting rather than through increases in value-added is both self-deceiving and self-defeating, yet not many seem to be aware that the remedy lies in productivity improvement, not in added production or sales turnover.

When Hong Kong's major competitors such as Korea and Taiwan are entering, or already in, the stage of innovation and technology-driven development, the days in which Hong Kong can still rely on factor-driven developments are limited. This, plus the emerging of China as an economic giant and the coming into effect of the North American Free Trade Agreement (NAFTA), should be sufficient cause for alarm in Hong Kong.

The Change in Investment Patterns

Many of us still believe that Hong Kong plays an important role in China's economic development and is thus almost indispensable to China. True, the moving of operations by Hong Kong's manufacturing sector to China, which started about a decade ago, was coupled with capital flow from Hong Kong to China and benefited China significantly: in 1990 alone, Hong Kong's investment in China comprised 18,851 projects, worth an estimated US$22.7 billion. In 1992, the number of projects increased to more than 30,000, and the amount of investment as recorded per agreements signed was over US$40 billion.

However, there has been a change in investment pattern or capital flow in recent years. Instead of a more or less one-way flow of capital from Hong Kong to the Mainland, China

Table 4.2   China's Estimated Investment in Hong Kong

	HK$ million
Bank of China Group's Assets (end of 1992)	530,000
Properties purchased, 1988–93	13,782
Market value of shares in listed companies (31 March 1993)	56,997
Total	600,779

has become the largest foreign investor in Hong Kong. I made an attempt last year to gauge the extent of China's investment in Hong Kong by estimating the assets of the Bank of China Group, land and property purchases made by China-owned companies in Hong Kong, and the market value of shares of public companies (owned by China-related entities) listed on the Stock Exchange of Hong Kong. They add up to about HK$600,779 million or more than US$77 billion, as shown in Table 4.2. This estimated amount includes neither all assets and investment held by the 1,000-member strong Hong Kong Chinese Enterprises Association (most of which are not listed on the local Stock Exchange) nor local companies acquired by China-owned entities after 31 March 1993.

This change from one-way investment, through the moving of manufacturing operations from Hong Kong to China, to a two-way flow of funds with China's increasing investment in Hong Kong is a clear indication of the fact that the notion of China's being dependent upon Hong Kong needs to be revised, if not thoroughly transformed. China is today Hong Kong's largest foreign investor, and Hong Kong's prosperity is more dependent upon China than China's on Hong Kong. The two economies are now so closely integrated that, even before 1997, they are practically using one system instead of two already.

In the meantime, there has been a change in the nature of Hong Kong's investment in China, from the expansion and extension of the manufacturing sector across the Shenzhen River, to involvement in infrastructure, such as the building of roads and power stations, and the retail trade. This signifies that Hong Kong has started to expand its service sectors to China. Such a change may help China raise its productivity in the related sectors, but whether or not they would lead to elevation or decline of productivity in these sectors in Hong Kong remains to be seen. How to raise productivity in these service sectors is already a challenge faced by Hong Kong's business community. Venturing into new grounds in China, though offering fresh opportunities, will also present new challenges to Hong Kong businessmen in their effort to make productivity improvements.

Three Main Problems

Although Hong Kong has prospered as a result of changes that have taken place since China started its economic reform, there are some obvious problems which must be reckoned with, amongst which three main ones are worth our attention.

The first problem, which has already been mentioned earlier, is the negative effect of moving manufacturing operations to China where factor costs, mainly labour and land, are much lower. Immediate gains in terms of profit due to lower production costs are made at the expense of Hong Kong's long-term industrial development. The availability of lower-cost production facilities outside Hong Kong means less need for Hong Kong to improve its own technology. We have seen that Hong Kong's manufacturing sector has been able to raise its productivity at a relatively fast pace compared with the other NIEs and emerging economies in Asia, but such productivity improvements may mainly be attributed to management ingenuity rather than technological innovations through Research and Development (R&D). In the long run, Hong Kong will be lingering behind its competitors in terms of its technological level and hence its new product development. With rising costs, the domestic industry will eventually become non-competitive. The GDP share of the manufacturing sector may be declining, but it still employs over half a million people—a very substantial portion of Hong Kong's labour force.

Unless we are convinced that Hong Kong can cope with the relocation of the present manufacturing sector workforce, and are prepared to see Hong Kong become a wholly service-oriented economy, investment in R&D to raise the technological level of the manufacturing industry should be a priority. Perhaps this is where the business community's future challenge lies.

Another main problem is the high rate of inflation which, if unabated, will sooner or later price Hong Kong out of competition *vis-à-vis* the other NIEs and emerging economies. Hong Kong has lost its leverage against inflation because of the linking of the Hong Kong dollar to the US dollar, resulting in negative interest rates and sky-rocketing real-estate prices. The purchase price of prime office space in the Central district was below HK$20,000 per square metre in 1985, but the latest market price is over HK$100,000 per square metre. As already mentioned earlier, the Hang Seng Index has risen to unprecedented heights, punctuated of course by dips, largely because people are reluctant to keep their money as bank deposits, subjecting themselves to penalization by negative interest rates. All these factors point to a bubble economy, the bursting of which would bring financial catastrophe, economic chaos, and social unrest. Arguments against the linked exchange system have been voiced time and again by numerous scholars and businessmen, but have for years fallen on deaf ears. It seems unlikely that the situation will undergo any changes in the foreseeable future. I am afraid that Hong Kong will eventually taste the bitter fruit.

The third problem is the consequence of the two described above. With its goods and services becoming non-competitive due to its technological inertia, and with its currency nailed to the linked exchange system, Hong Kong may cease to be an economically viable entity in this highly competitive world and become more and more dependent upon China for its survival. By that time, should Hong Kong's role as a financial centre be taken over by places such as Singapore, Shanghai, or Taipei, it would have completed its historical mission in China's economic development, and whether or not it remained prosperous would be of little consequence to China.

During the last decade, ever since Hong Kong started to invest in China and the Hong Kong dollar became linked to US currency, the prosperity enjoyed by Hong Kong and China's rapid economic growth have been attributed to the integration of the two economies. Increases in the volume of products and in business profits earned through offshore manufacturing operations as manifested by significant rises in Hong Kong's re-exports, coupled with an appreciation of real-estate values and surges in the Hang Seng Index, have created a euphoric atmosphere in Hong Kong, because many people have seen their wealth multiply at an unprecedented pace. Of course, due credit must be given to the business community for making such things happen, and there is no denying that the track-record of the past decade more than demonstrates the foresight and wisdom of Hong Kong industrialists and businessmen alike.

However, while the high rate of inflation has been the concern of many, few members of the business community seem worried by the other two problems mentioned above—maybe this is because few people think about the long-term future of Hong Kong as long as profits keep rolling in. Maybe we are already so deeply addicted to the soothing effect of the linked exchange system that any criticism thereof is either discarded outright or treated with disdain. Maybe productivity is something which had better be left to the Hong Kong Productivity Council. After all, Hong Kong's productivity has been improving, which shows that since its inception, about twenty-five years ago, the Hong Kong Productivity Council has done a good job. But we would be committing a grave error if we did not look seriously into the consequences of stagnant productivity growth in some of the service industries which are vital to Hong Kong's future prosperity, if not survival. In the final analysis, the world has become a global village, and Hong Kong, presently at the hub of a vibrant regional economy, can not afford to be complacent. We need to face the problems and tackle them one by one in order to maintain and sustain our present position. Let us not forget that an even more challenging future awaits us all, and that the key to prosperity is productivity.

Appendix to Chapter 4

A Note on the Constant Prices Computation

Hong Kong does not have, in its national accounts, value-added by economic activities at constant prices. Hence national account value-added of the various sectors, such as manufacturing, construction, and trade, will need to be converted to constant prices by a set of deflators. Deflated value-added may be derived by means of double deflation, with outputs and inputs deflated separately by two kinds of deflators compiled from output and input prices respectively. But this is not practical since Hong Kong has neither a producer price index nor a wholesale price index.

An alternative method is to use the unit value index for domestic exports to deflate value-added of the manufacturing sector, because Hong Kong exports most of its manufactured products. But, since Hong Kong's domestic exports are declining and re-exports are becoming more important, using such a deflator would present a highly distorted picture. Also, export prices do not satisfy the requirements of producer prices because of export margins, insurance, and freight.

Hence, for the manufacturing sector, a simpler method of using the production indexes as deflators is employed. In addition, an attempt has been made to use the volume index for gross output as an extrapolator in determining the value-added in constant prices terms from the base year figures. However, in the present paper, no such extrapolation has been made, because after trying with the extrapolator, the outcome seems to be biased toward the high side and rather unrealistic.

The deflators used in the service sectors differ from sector to sector. They include the relevant unit value indexes of imports and exports, consumer price index and private consumption expenditure price deflator for the trade, transport, and communication sectors; and consumer price index, Hang Seng Index and building-cost index for the finance and business services sector.

Important Note:
Due to data constraint and crude method of deflation, the productivity indexes of Hong Kong at the sectoral level in this paper are very preliminary, for reference only, and not to be quoted. It is hereby explicitly stated that the figures attached to this paper are of an indicative nature only.

Note on Sources:
The sources of data for the figures and Table 4.1 are as follows: 'Comparative Information on Productivity Levels and Changes in APO Member Countries 1992 and 1993', *Asian Productivity Organization*, Tokyo, 1993 and 1994; *Key Indicators of Developing Asian and Pacific Countries*, Asian Development Bank: Manila, 1993 and 1994; *National Accounts Statistics: Main Aggregates and Detailed Tables*, United Nations (various years); *Hong Kong Monthly Digest of Statistics, Census and Statistical Department*, Hong Kong, 1991 to 1994. Table 4.2 is compiled from data contained in 'China's Investment in Hong Kong' by George Shen, in *The Other Hong Kong Report 1993*, Choi Po-king and Ho Lok-sang (eds.), The Chinese University Press: Hong Kong, 1993.

5 Expectations and Challenges in School Education

RITA FAN

THE VALUE of studying history, I have been told, lies in the analysis of past events which may enable us to anticipate what is ahead; and the lessons learnt in the past may help us steer clear of similar mistakes and be that much wiser in our future endeavours. This series of Hong Kong lectures, focusing on the ten transition years between 1984 and 1994 may be viewed as a stock-taking and analytical exercise on the one hand, and as an opportunity for projecting into the future on the other.

During the last decade, I think the main feature in the development in school education has been the realization that education can only be meaningful if the student benefits from the process. A more student-centred approach, emphasizing individual needs and progress is needed. The importance is now recognized of allowing schools a higher degree of autonomy to develop activities and teaching methods more suited to their students' needs. Parents should have more choice and participation in their children's education as far as possible. Teachers should be better equipped for their work—which has become increasingly demanding—through better training. All these improvements are resource-intensive. However, if the community wants quality, we have to invest accordingly. With more of the taxpayer's money devoted to education, the education community is expected to be more accountable.

In this lecture, I shall attempt to recount some of the recommendations made by the Education Commission in our Reports IV and V, and the reasons behind them. It is at best a sketchy account. I shall start with the 'nine years free and compulsory education' which was implemented more than two decades ago. Nearly all the Education Commission's recommendations in the two reports mentioned above were aimed at improving these nine years of universal education.

Nine Years of Universal Education

The implementation of the 'nine years of free and compulsory education' in 1979 had the desirable effect of improving the overall education level of the population. In 1982, 51 per cent of the population completed secondary education; by 1992, the corresponding figure was 60.9 per cent.[1] It also offered the opportunity for the abolition of three examinations, at Primary 1, Primary 6, and Form 3 respectively,[2] thereby reducing examination pressure for students at these levels. The requirement by many schools for six year olds to take an examination for admission to Primary 1 was stopped in 1983 and the Primary 1 Admission System[3] came into effect. The Secondary School Entrance Examination, which caused considerable pressure for many Primary 6 students, was replaced by the Secondary School Places Allocation (SSPA)[4] in 1978. The Junior Secondary Education Assessment System (JSEA) was revised in 1988 so that Form 3 students did not have to sit a public test, but those who wished to further their studies were allocated a place. By 1991, over 93

[1] See *Hong Kong and Economic Trends*, 1982–92, Hong Kong: Census & Statistics Department, p. 82.

[2] The Primary 1 test was given to a child at about 6 years old. The Primary 6 examination was given to students of about 12 years old. The Form 3 examination was taken by students of around 15 years old.

[3] In principle, all primary students should study in a school nearby. The selection of students by schools is based on a point system. For example points are awarded to an applicant whose parents and/or siblings are teachers/past students/current students of the school. Points are also awarded if the applicant's parents belong to the same religious body as the sponsoring body of the school. Admission is based on the number of points an applicant is given.

[4] Internal assessment at Primary 5 and Primary 6, scaled by the Academic Aptitude Test, enabled the division of students into 5 bands, with Band 1 students being academically the most able. A random allocation of one number per student is done by computer. The result is two students, both in Band 1, can be allocated numbers 1 and 99. The student with no. 1 will be given the choice of school in his region (geographical area) first. The student with no. 99 has to wait until the 98 students in front of him have chosen. In this way, the ability of the student and his choice (usually this is the choice of his parents) are both taken into account, but their effect is to some extent neutralized by the random allocation of numbers. The use of the SSPA is intended to reduce the pressure of public examination.

per cent of Form 3 leavers were automatically offered places in Form 4, or on craft courses.

The implementation of universal education in Hong Kong and the introduction of these new allocation methods were welcomed by the community at that time. However, as time went by, problems began to appear. Teachers had to instruct students of a wider range of abilities in the same class using a curriculum not yet adopted for this change. Bright students got bored when the teacher slowed down to allow others to catch up. Slow learners lost confidence in their studies. Behavioural problems became more pronounced in class and at school. Students whose self-esteem suffered due to their academic performance at school became easy prey for bad elements in society and turned to drugs and crime. Parents who had a keen interest in their children's education began to realize that their choice over which schools their children could attend was very limited, particularly at the secondary school admission level. Many parents complained that chance, through random allocation of a number by the computer, could affect the choice of school more than the parents' wishes. Some commentators believed that the abolition of the Secondary School Entrance Examination and the introduction of the SSPA led to a drop in the standard of English of primary school students. With the removal of English from the centrally administered Academic Aptitude Test,[5] some claimed that primary schools no longer placed an emphasis on English, and this was manifested in the exceptionally low standard of English amongst some Form 1 students. This meant that secondary schools had to devote more time to English to allow their students to catch up. Employers also complained that there was a general drop in the educational levels of secondary school-leavers particularly in their English-language abilities. All these issues were extensively discussed by the Education Commission during the years 1986 to 1992, and recommendations were put forward.

A point worth noting here is that in introducing new education policies in response to changing needs and public expectations, there are always some ensuing problems. Some

---

[5] The AAT covers verbal and numerical reasoning. Students take this test in the second term of Primary 5 and the first term of Primary 6. The results are used to scale the internal assessments given to students by the schools.

of them could be foreseen—teaching a class of wide-ranging abilities, for example, with a curriculum not adapted for this purpose—but were left aside for the sake of expediency and lack of resources, whilst other problems could not be foreseen—for example, the apparent lack of parental choice, which rendered responsible parents feeling helpless and frustrated. Yet, popular demand sometimes forces decisions to be taken quickly and before we are ready. We simply have to accept the challenges presented by subsequent problems, and take positive steps to deal with them.

Improving the Quality of Education

After the provision of universal education in schools, the emphasis naturally turned towards the quality of education. The latter is measured by how much the student benefited from the education process.

Curriculum Development and Teaching Methods

Students possess different aptitudes and interests. A suitable curriculum and an appropriate teaching method can facilitate learning. However, it would be expecting too much of one curriculum to be suitable for each and every student in our system. The same applies to teaching methods. To enable healthy development of suitable curricula, the Curriculum Development Institute (CDI) was proposed, with staff drawn from inside and outside the civil service with a high degree of financial flexibility through a one-line vote. The purpose of the CDI was to develop resource materials and manage resource centres to assist teachers. School-based support services, including remedial teaching, guidance, and counselling, were to be strengthened by additional funding to cater to the needs of individual students, albeit to a limited extent. The establishment of practical schools were proposed for students unmotivated towards schoolwork, and Skills Opportunity Schools were suggested for students with severe learning problems. Together, these schools were intended to provide a total of 2,850 places for students. The class size would be smaller, ranging from twenty to thirty, to enable teachers to give more personal attention to each student. All of these recommendations reflected a central theme: students should be taught in ways appropriate to their abilities.

Medium of Instruction

The majority of students in the education system today follow the common-core curriculum. However, in order to benefit from their studies, they should learn in a language in which they are well-versed. The Education Commission argued long and hard for nearly two years over the issue of which language to use in education. We agreed that conducting classes in the students' mother tongue would probably best enable them to understand their studies. However, there were students who could learn equally well in English. Should we insist that all students learn in Chinese (the spoken form being Cantonese in Hong Kong) and thereby remove from the small group of students who could learn well in English the choice of doing so? Whilst everyone was keen to promote mother-tongue teaching and learning, it was debatable whether the choice of learning in another language should be taken away from students, their parents, the teachers, and the schools. It was suggested, at one stage of our deliberations, that schools be examined on their ability to use English as their medium of instruction. The notion was that teachers would have to pass a qualifying test, and students who wanted to join those schools at Form 1 should have already reached a certain standard in English. This met with strong objections from some members of the Commission. I personally thought that while in theory it might sound feasible, in practice it could be rather difficult to execute. Moreover, it also removed the element of choice. I believed we should have sufficient confidence, not only in the professional ethics of our teaching profession and school management to place the interest of the students first in making their choice, but also in the love and care of parents towards their children to choose a school with a medium of instruction that their children could manage. Until we were proved wrong, I doubted if we should contemplate the 'testing' method. Eventually the Commission suggested a method which strongly favoured the use of Chinese as the teaching language in secondary schools, but preserved the right of choice for parents and schools. However, it was agreed that if our suggested method was proved to be insufficient for achieving the objective, the Education Department would exert strong guidance.

The 'Good' School

Throughout the Commission's deliberation on the language of instruction, one item kept coming back into our discussion: the questions of the 'good' school, or the 'élite' school. One of the strong reasons for many secondary schools to refrain from using Chinese as the medium of instruction was the fear that these schools would be seen by parents as inferior. As a result, students joining these schools would come from band 5 or, at best, band 4. Teachers in these schools would face a heavier work load since band 5 students, being less able academically, would need more tuition. The Hong Kong Certificate of Education examination results of these students, five years later, would also reflect the quality of the intake, and students from these schools gaining places in tertiary institutions would be fewer. This, in turn, would cause the school's reputation to drop, and make it even less attractive to parents and students. The School Management Committee would not be pleased. The Principal would be pressured on all sides by the School Management Committee, the teachers, and the parents. Whilst well-established schools endeavoured to maintain their reputations, newly established schools made every effort to become 'good' schools by ensuring better public examination results. One of the consequences of this was that the workload in schools remained very heavy even though the examinations at Primary 1, 6, and Form 3 had been removed. The less able students often received less, not more, attention from the teachers, who had to keep in sight the achievement of their students in the School Certificate Examination.

One had to ask whether this was an appropriate way to identify 'good' schools. If a school starts with band 5 students, and these students achieve average results in the public examinations, is this school doing better or worse than another school which takes in band 1 students, and their students achieve above average results? I think the first school is doing better. A more appropriate 'ruler' for the 'good' school is to measure the progress made by the students, rather than merely comparing public examination results.

Attainment Targets and Related Assessments

If an academically weak student is continually compared with his brighter counterparts, his efforts and hard work can hardly be reflected in his marks. He is always lagging behind, and thus receives little reinforcement for his efforts. It would be much more desirable if each student were judged on his own merits, and then informed of the progress achieved. This is why the Education Commission proposed the framework of attainment targets and related assessments. I was mindful that this would eventually lead to a change in the attitude towards teaching and learning. Teachers would be more concerned about the progress of each individual student, rather than merely the bright students. Students would be comparing their most recent achievements with what they had done in the past, rather than only with one another. In this way, the education process stretches the student's mind and potential to the fullest extent. A young person will be more likely to achieve higher levels if he is reinforced by the knowledge that he has done well at the last level. This target-related assessment enables the student to understand his own progress, which will give him momentum to move further ahead.

This recommendation of the Commission was accepted as government policy. But, as we all know, its implementation is suffering a few hiccups. It is not an easy task, and I salute all those who are committed to putting it into practice. I sincerely hope that this worthy concept will not be lost in the maze of politics and resource limitations.

The Effect of Expansion of Tertiary Education on Schools

One of the main reasons put forth to explain the emphasis on examination results in secondary schools was the fierce competition for the limited number of degree places in local tertiary institutions. In 1984 there were only enough places for 3 per cent of the 17 to 20 age group. This was expanded to 7 per cent in 1989, but was still not enough to ease the pressure felt by students and the schools. During the discussion on the drop in language abilities of secondary school-leavers, quite a few commentators claimed, and I think with some justification, that students were spending too much time on other subjects (particularly science subjects) in order to get better results to improve their admission chances, thereby neglecting English and Chinese. Some principals even felt that secondary schools were being led by the nose by the universities. Between 1994 and 1995 the number of degree places is set to increase to accommodate 18 per cent of school-leavers; this will have the effect of relaxing the competitive regime. However, students should take this opportunity to enhance their personal development and widen their scope of interest and knowledge, rather than just having a relaxing time by default.

Parental Choice and Participation

As I mentioned earlier, some parents were frustrated at their lack of say in choosing their children's schools. This is particularly difficult to accept when a child does well in primary school, but fails to secure a place in the secondary school of the same sponsoring body, as a result of the computer allocation exercise; whilst a classmate of theirs, known to be less able academically, is able to continue in the secondary section of the same body. I had parents coming to see me in tears to ask for some remedy to the situation. Whilst I had every sympathy for them, I was unable to offer any real assistance. I do feel strongly however that parents should be offered more choice. The Direct Subsidy Scheme (DSS),[6] in a small way, may offer another option for parents. Schools in this scheme enjoy more flexibility and freedom in their curriculum and in the way resources are used. For the moment, there are only private schools and international schools in this group, but the scheme does offer the potential for any public-sector school (except government schools) to consider joining. I look forward to a time when, encouraged by the success of existing DSS schools, more schools apply to join DSS, thereby offering parents more choices.

Perhaps this is an appropriate point for me to put in a word on 'élitism'. The introduction of the DSS had been accused of reintroducing élitism into education. It was argued that

[6] DSS schools are outside the SSPA system. They enjoy a higher degree of autonomy and are responsible for their own finances and management. Parents apply to DSS schools directly and the schools select their own students.

since the DSS allowed schools to charge a higher fee for a better staff-to-student ratio and above-standard facilities, it made these schools accessible only to rich kids, thereby depriving poorer pupils of the opportunity. The main flaw in this argument is the assumption that élitism can only be achieved by deprivation of the masses. This is not true. Universal education offers every child the opportunity to be educated, but it does not rule out diversification in the education system to accommodate children of different aptitude, nor does it rule out 'choice'. Indeed, choice is sometimes free, and sometimes it carries a price. If some parents are prepared to pay extra for a certain type of education—we should not simplify matters into 'rich' against 'poor', nor forget the possibility of scholarships and bursaries—why shouldn't these parents be allowed the choice? Surely, we are not such a totalitarian society that everyone has to be reduced to the lowest common denominator? As you can see, I have some strong views on this, and no doubt, people on the opposite side have equally strong views. It is probably sufficient for me to state my opinions and say that I consider a certain amount of so-called 'élitism' to be necessary in education for developing our future leaders, but this must not be done at the expense of our less able children. A balance is needed. The challenge is to find the right pivot point at every stage of development.

I believe most people will agree that the education process is most effective and beneficial for the students if close co-operation, based on mutual understanding, exists between schools and parents. To establish this kind of relationship, there must first be communications between the two parties. Parents should have an idea of how their children spend the day at school and be able to offer suggestions to the school on the education of their children. It is also important for parents to be able to identify with the school's educational principles and reinforce them where possible during out-of-school hours. In this way, parents feel a sense of responsibility towards the education of their children. Principals and teachers should be prepared to talk with parents and help them understand the school's methods. Schools should try to involve parents in school activities and should be receptive to feedback and suggestions from parents. However, as with many things in life, this does not often happen in reality.

Some parents take no interest in their children's education, whilst other parents want to be involved, but receive no encouragement from the school. Parents have very little say in what happens in schools, and are the least organized group of 'indirect' consumers. This is not a satisfactory situation.

Two recent developments have, to a certain extent, addressed this problem. The first was the introduction of the School Management Initiative whereby parents' representatives are given seats on the School Management Committee. The second was the establishment of a Committee on Home–School Cooperation which promotes the formation of a Parent–Teacher Association, as well as the idea of cooperation and communication between schools and parents. The latter committee is provided with funds to carry out its work. I expect these developments to be conducive to parent participation, which is such a vital element in education.

Improving the Quality of the Teaching Profession

When the Commission considered its proposals on improving the quality of education in schools, it was obvious to all of us that teachers were the most significant factor in our quest for better education. So the working environment, promotion prospects, teacher training and induction, professional upgrading, the status of the teaching profession, and the ability to attract young people of high calibre into the profession were all tackled in Commission Report No. 5. Our recommendations were described by the media as 'Education Rose Garden' because they were expensive and would take a long time to complete. Effects of our proposal would probably take more than five years after its implementation to be felt, but at least we have started.

Accountability and the Aims in Education

Our taxpayers contribute a substantial amount of money to education every year. Are they being given their money's worth? I doubt if anyone can answer that question. However, a system of authority matched with responsibility and accountability is being set up through the School Management Initiative project. In general terms, schools will be given more discretion in planning and implementation, with the Education Department less involved in the details, but playing an overall monitoring role. However, the schools are also expected to accept more responsibility and be more accountable to the public. As this evolves, school management will become more professional, more sensitive to community needs, and more ready to take independent decisions and be prepared to explain such decisions. While this is basically a Hong Kong government initiative, I agree that it is a move in the right direction, but the challenge it places on the schools must not be underestimated.

With hindsight, I think accountability in school education was probably in the back of my mind when the Commission decided to tackle the Aims of Education in Schools. In my very first meeting of the Commission, one member innocently asked what objectives we were trying to achieve in Education. A full-scale debate ensued, but no conclusion was reached. So I welcomed the opportunity to resume that debate when the Education Commission Report No. 5 was completed. The Commission published a booklet entitled 'School Education in Hong Kong: A Statement of Aims' for public consultation in October 1992. I am most grateful to the current Education Commission and, in particular, the Chairman for finalizing 'A Statement of Aims'. I hope this document will serve as a useful reference for the education community, enabling them to evaluate their own performance and be accountable to the public.

The Next Ten Years

As time goes by, the actual impact of the decisions taken in education during the last decade will unfold. The course taken in implementing some of the decisions may twist and turn, as a result of public pressure and political considerations, and the wisdom of these decisions will be judged accordingly. Looking ahead, I should like to offer a few thoughts.

Education as a Stabilizing Factor and a Basis for Economic Development

The Hong Kong community has always attached a high value to Education because we believe a better educated population is the key to a civilized society and economic growth. On an individual level, education offers an accepted route for personal advancement and upward mobility for the family. So long as this is attainable through education, there is hope. There are plenty of examples of success—these help to relieve dissatisfaction and frustration towards the current systems, thereby strengthening the stability of the community. On a wider level, the continuous development, or merely the maintenance of Hong Kong as an international business centre, requires the support of a well-educated workforce. Education must continue to play this role in the next decade. It is vital for Hong Kong to retain its status in international trade, and to use our China connection to enhance this status. Our education system will therefore have to cater for the language needs of our students: English standards must not be allowed to fall; training in Mandarin has to be strengthened; Chinese writing skills have to be mastered. Students should develop a wider outlook with an open attitude towards unfamiliar ideas and ways, so that they can take advantage of changes, and grow with new developments. If we are to keep Hong Kong visible on the world map, we must preserve the Hong Kong spirit in our young people, and education is the process which will achieve this.

Resourcing in Education

Money is not all-powerful, but without money very little can be done. Sufficient funding is the prerequisite for the maintenance and improvement of standards in education. Over the last twenty years, a substantial portion (ranging between 14 and 20 per cent) of total public expenditure has been devoted to education (see Table 5.1).

This provides indisputable evidence of the government and the community's commitment towards education. However, if we are to respond effectively and efficiently to public expectations, and have sufficient resources to tackle the challenges ahead, I do think it is necessary to raise the share of education in the total public expenditure from the 1993/4 rate of 16.2 per cent and the 1994/5 rate of 16.5 per cent, to 18 per cent. This can be achieved by increasing the allocation gradually over a period of time. If we wish to implement the proposals of the Education Commission, if we wish to have whole-day schooling in the primary section, if we wish the quality of kindergarten education to improve, if we wish to

Table 5.1 Education Expenditure over the last Twenty Years

Financial Year	Total Expenditure (HK$ million)	Expenditure in Education (HK$ million)	Percentage of Total Expenditure
72–73	3,875	711	18.3
73–74	5,061	1,011	20.0
74–75	6,692	1,164	17.4
75–76	6,576	1,290	19.6
76–77	7,355	1,431	19.5
77–78	9,168	1,655	18.0
78–79	12,122	1,967	16.2
79–80	15,619	2,475	15.9
80–81	22,058	3,358	15.2
81–82	29,383	4,172	14.2
82–83	35,684	5,105	14.3
83–84	38,596	5,758	14.9
84–85	39,882	6,951	17.4
85–86	43,444	7,558	17.4
86–87	47,930	8,771	18.3
87–88	53,636	9,172	17.1
88–89	64,799	11,340	17.5
89–90	81,945	13,029	15.9
90–91	95,198	16,088	16.9
91–92	108,012	18,794	17.4
92–93*	127,300	22,005	17.3
93–94**	156,610	25,365	16.2

* Revised estimate
** Draft estimates
(*Source*: Extracted from figures in various budgets)

phase out floating classes,[7] if we wish special education to enjoy healthy development, if we wish to provide an environment in which students can really benefit from education and learn, how to think, learn, and perform, we have no alternative but to invest more money. I made the call for

---

[7] Classes of students which do not have a classroom assigned to them on a permanent basis move to different rooms for each lesson.

more investments in 1992, and I ask for your indulgence in repeating it again today.

Accountability and Professionalism in Education

To reinforce the confidence of government officials and tax-payers that the resources devoted to education are used in a cost-effective manner, accountability in education cannot be overemphasized. Accountability goes hand-in-hand with professionalism. A self-respecting professional always asks himself whether he has offered the client his best service. In education, the clients are the students. To satisfy the client, and also one's own standards, educationalists should ensure that the students under their care really benefit from the education process. Increasing public demand for accountability is already the trend in the more developed countries; the call for professionalism amongst teachers in Hong Kong started a decade ago and is gathering momentum. If our teaching profession responds to the challenge of accountability, teachers will be seen and respected as professionals. Better training, attractive salary scales, and favourable promotion prospects all contribute to the upgrading of a profession. However, these conditions have to be coupled with professional ethics, devotion to the work, and care for the students, so that the status of a profession can be firmly established. No one in education should ever forget that there is only one reason for the system, the staff, and the infra-structure, and that is the students. So in everything we do, every move we make, we shall be assessed on how much the students have benefited.

The Politicizing of Education

There are plenty of examples in the Western world, of education becoming a political issue. Education is, in fact, the easy prey of politicians. Because so many voters are concerned about their children's schooling, education often becomes a contentious electioneering issue. Once elected, in order to fulfil election promises, changes are made to the system, which correct the perceived problem, but often go too far. I call this phenomenon the 'pendulum' effect—in adjusting the slant, too much force is used, so that the pendulum swings to the other side, probably further away from the middle than before. In Hong Kong the same will happen, if it has not happened already. I can only hope that local politicians will be prepared to implement changes gradually, so that chances of missing the mark will be reduced, and everyone can catch up with the momentum.

The Effect of 1997 on Education

I do not feel that the transition in 1997 and the formation of the Hong Kong Special Administrative Region government should necessarily have a great impact on education in Hong Kong. Articles 136, 137, 144, 148, and 149 of the Basic Law (see Appendix for exact quotations) ensure the continuation of the current system and practices. However, although I am not worried does not mean that other people are not worried. The fact that the Basic Law virtually promises the continuation of the present system and the preservation of academic freedom does not rule out potential attempts to bring the Hong Kong system into line with that of China. There are some who would say that, since we followed the British system when we were under British rule, we should follow the Chinese system when we return to China. To this, my response is: if you believe in 'one country, two systems',[8] you should realize that the Chinese government has no intention of imposing their system in Hong Kong. We should allow our present education system to evolve and improve in line with the needs of our community.

Conclusion

Change in the education system is inevitable. As society evolves, education must respond appropriately and effectively to changing demands. Hong Kong, as an international business centre, will probably face more pressure and challenges than other countries. Our citizens need to be equipped with better and faster abilities to analyse and respond. This is what education is supposed to do for our young people. Let us try to do it wisely, with vision and empathy.

---

[8] After 1 July 1997 Hong Kong will become for 50 years a Special Administrative Region under the sovereignty of China.

Appendix to Chapter 5

The Basic Law of the Hong Kong Special Administrative Region of the People's Republic of China—Extracts relating to Education

Article 136
On the basis of the previous educational system, the government of the Hong Kong Special Administrative Region shall, on its own, formulate policies on the development and improvement of education, including policies regarding the educational system and its administration, the language of instruction, the allocation of funds, the examination system, the system of academic awards, and the recognition of educational qualifications.

Community organizations and individuals may, in accordance with law, run educational undertakings of various kinds in the Hong Kong Special Administrative Region.

Article 137
Educational institutions of all kinds may retain their autonomy and enjoy academic freedom. They may continue to recruit staff and use teaching materials from outside the Hong Kong Special Administrative Region. Schools run by religious organizations may continue to provide religious education, including courses in religion.

Students shall enjoy freedom of choice of educational institutions, and freedom to pursue their education outside the Hong Kong Special Administrative Region.

Article 144
The government of the Hong Kong Special Administrative Region shall maintain the policy previously practised in Hong Kong in respect of subventions for non-governmental organizations in fields such as education, medicine and health, culture, art, recreation, sports, social welfare, and social work. Staff members previously serving in subvented organizations in Hong Kong may remain in their employment in accordance with the previous system.

Article 148
The relationship between non-governmental organizations in fields such as education, science, technology, culture, art, sports, the professions, medicine and health, labour, social welfare, and social work, as well as religious organizations in the Hong Kong Special Administrative Region and their counterparts on the Mainland, shall be based on the principles of non-subordination, non-interference, and mutual respect.

Article 149
Non-governmental organizations in fields such as education, science, technology, culture, art, sports, the professions, medicine and health, labour, social welfare, and social work, as well as religious organizations in the Hong Kong Special Administrative Region may maintain and develop relations with their counterparts in foreign countries and regions, and with relevant international organizations. They may, as required, use the name 'Hong Kong, China' in the relevant activities.

6 Economic Interactions: China *vis-à-vis* Hong Kong

STEVEN N. S. CHEUNG

IN 1988 I took Milton Friedman on a tour of China. During that visit he was mightily impressed by the developments and changes which had come about in that country. Since then, Milton has reiterated over and again that the key difference between China's sparkling economic performance and the lack-lustre showing by countries in Eastern Europe and the former Soviet Union is the presence of Hong Kong, right on China's doorstep.

Friedman's argument would be convincing, except for a glaring counter example: the Czech Republic, at a comparable stage of its economic reform, has been doing better than China, and we don't find a Hong Kong on its frontier. What the Czech government did was systematically to privatize its economy, lock, stock, and barrel. After three or four years of this, if we compare the situation with China in the early 1980s, there is no question that the Czechs are ahead. This confirms what I have argued all along: private-property rights rank first, when it comes to economic growth and advancing economic activity.

There is another issue: speaking for myself, I do not believe democracy would work without a well-defined constitution, or unless there exists a system in which individual and private-property rights are well defined and fully protected. However, if you give democracy to a society in chaos, matters are likely to grow worse. And one of the reasons the Chinese economy has been doing so well, I am sorry to say— since my friend Martin Lee[1] is not here—is precisely this. I think one key factor why China is ahead of Eastern Europe, Russia, et al., is because Beijing puts economic reform ahead of political reform.

---

[1] Martin Lee is a member of the Legislative Council and Leader of the United Democratic Party.

Political reform will come one day, but at this stage it is difficult to see how, without some kind of 'benevolent dictatorship', things could work. And the Czech experience, in some sense, also confirms this view. I agree with Friedman that Hong Kong is very important to modernization in China. However, I don't think it is the most important: I would put it second. I think privatization is the most important.

In 1981, I wrote a little pamphlet which argued that China would go capitalist. I predicted that China would adopt some private-property system, with a rapidly expanding market economy. At that time everybody thought I was crazy. But if you look at that book now—it is still available in the bookstores—the thing reads as if history had been written in advance. I am so proud of my 1981 prediction that I wish I could do as well in the stock market!

That little book had many things to say about the influence of Hong Kong. I pointed out that if China kept the door open, Hong Kong could not help but demonstrate the superiority of capitalism over communism/socialism, and people in Beijing would have a hard time denying the success of our market economy. Remember the similar culture, the same race, the same Chinese-speaking people, most of whom were in fact originally refugees from China. I always joke that Hong Kong Chinese are better than mainland Chinese because they survived sharks when swimming out here, but other than that they do not have any special talent. With Hong Kong so close to China, and culture and language the same, it is difficult to imagine that (in my economic language) the cost of transaction or the cost of information will not be sharply reduced if China keeps the door open.

I believe this reduction of information cost matters a great deal. In due course, the long-held belief in the superiority of communism/socialism would collapse, with the glaring example of Hong Kong standing one neighbourhood away from China, particularly since so many people have been coming in and out since 1979.

So that is one important factor, in which Hong Kong provides an informational impetus for change in China. But there are other factors as well. Human capital, technological know-how, and particularly financial expertise—all the resources China requires for modernization—Hong Kong possesses in abundance. And then you have the window to the outside world—middlemen in trading, import–export, technology transfer—all are important to economic development in China. If you look carefully, you will be able to trace in recent Chinese policies Hong Kong blueprints, stuff they copy pretty thoroughly, though I cannot think of any case which ended up being better. For example, the selling of land based on long leases was copied from Hong Kong. I remember around 1986 or so, some Chinese officials invited me to talk about selling land, and they clearly had Hong Kong in mind. Another thing they tried to emulate was auctioning for government projects. This has never caught on in China—to do so would take away too many corruption opportunities, I presume.

So, no doubt about it, Hong Kong has been instrumental in economic development in China. Had China not opened up, Hong Kong's options would have been very limited. But with China opening up and transforming into a market economy (or what I prefer to call a system of private-property rights), people in Hong Kong are bound to make a lot of money. In the United States it is said that for every seven persons there is one service middleman. So if you look at the population in China, everybody in Hong Kong could be kept employed. Think what a tremendous break this is both for Hong Kong and for China. Of course, having a common language is a huge advantage, for if you put Hong Kong next to Russia it would not do them that much good.

Hong Kong's partnership with China has been working well, and there is no reason to think the symbiosis will not continue. In 1983, the 1997 issue came up, which brought about the yoyo effect in the stock market. But I was optimistic. I gave up university housing and bought my own house; I wish I had bought more. The partnership between Hong Kong and China has a good future, and it is worth gambling on. But before we proceed to talk in more concrete terms about what lies ahead, I would like to expound a global view, and sketch a world scenario which I think is in the process of unfolding.

Communism, as we all know (with the exceptions of North Korea and Cuba) has collapsed. The result is that former communist countries have all been trying to open up to the world. I think it was in 1991 that I calculated that as a result (and because of another factor discussed below) the world suddenly found itself with an additional 1.5 billion labourers available for capitalists to 'exploit'. The supply of cheap labour had jumped ten-fold in short order. Assuming that the trend continued, I think today it should be close to two billion.

This sudden and sharp increase in cheap labour does not come from former communist countries alone. Under the pressure of increasing competition, other developing countries such as Mexico, Latin America, India, Indochina, Indonesia, and so on, all open wide their doors, smiling, and waving their hands. The force of this development has hit many countries without them fully knowing why. I always wonder why leaders such as John Major in the United Kingdom, or Bush or Clinton in the United States, or the Canadians and Australians, did not see this tidal wave of cheap labour coming. It is sad that even today they do not seem to realize the deep trouble they are in.

What does this mean economically? It means that manufacturing countries which have been employing expensive labour and enjoying high social welfare programmes are going to have a difficult time. In Toronto, Canada, for example, skilled labour costs C$25 an hour; then you have to add on top social benefits, vacations—all those welfare programmes and retirement benefits. It comes to close on C$70 an hour for skilled labour. Hire a comparable man in Russia, and he would only cost you US$15 (C$20.85) a month!

Another aspect of the scenario is that because communism took so long to die, a large part of the world is going to require rebuilding. You have China, you have the former Soviet Union, Eastern Europe, Vietnam, and so on—all these countries will need a lot of reconstruction. Go to Shenzhen and take a look. Twelve years ago it was practically nothing. Now Shenzhen's skyline—at night when you can't see how dirty it is—looks like Manhattan. Try it sometime: it's an amazing sight. This development will continue for the next twenty or thirty years, during which time all those backward cities have to be improved, and all those industries have to be modernized. This gives rise to an enormous demand for financing worldwide, now and for years to come.

The following conclusion must then follow, as I noted in a 1988 article which landed me in a lot of trouble. It was, I think, in *Capital Magazine* that I have this piece with the title—I am sorry to repeat it with my Japanese friends sitting down there—'Japan is Finished'. At that time Japanese stocks were selling at historical highs and property prices were going stratospheric. I didn't really believe it myself, of course, otherwise I would have sold Japanese stocks short and made a fortune. Again, when I was interviewed by an Ontario radio station about three years ago, when high unemployment was haunting the country, the reporter asked: 'Professor Cheung, when do you expect Canada, and Ontario, to recover?' I said, 'Never!' I hate to rub it in. I think there may be mild recoveries in Canada, the United States, England, or Japan, but economic activity will not be as robust as before—not for a long time. You see, to cheapen labour sharply is politically impossible, for how are you going to persuade your voters to take a pay cut down to 5 per cent of what they have been getting? Countries with strong labour unions and massive welfare programmes, such as Canada and Sweden, are going to be hard hit for years.

A great many people in the advanced-developed countries, I am sure, find comfort in thinking that high technology will save their economies, because the textbooks seem to teach that cheap labour means low technology. This is not necessarily so; and the Chinese experience suggests that—self-inflicted restrictions on the importation of parts notwithstanding—the adoption of high technology is happening much faster than was thought possible ten years ago. Of course, we do not expect China to manufacture jumbo jets or Ferraris in the foreseeable future, or rush to do research on recombinant DNA, but, by and large, the rule is that, if it is profitable to adopt high technology, it will be done quickly. We must remember that the cost of high technology has dropped sharply over the past quarter of a century.

Not even protectionism will be able to stop the cheap-labour surge. It's not a matter of labour being a little cheaper, or about supply going up by 5 to 10 per cent. We are talking something like a 10- or 20-fold increase. It will be difficult for a high-wage country to compete, or to prohibit the importation of goods manufactured by its own citizens investing abroad. In due course, high labour-cost economies would start falling apart, unless certain things happened—

you would have to cut wages sharply, and cancel a lot of top-heavy welfare programmes. But none of these things is likely to happen.

Four years ago I was in Taiwan talking to this beautiful lady Financial Minister, who embarrassed a lot of people, if you remember, by standing up during the Chinese national anthem in Beijing. Well, she is smart—certainly smarter than Clinton or Major—and she saw what was going to happen to Taiwan. She saw what was coming but didn't know what to do: 'What are we going to do? Are we going to allow all our industries to move to China or Vietnam, or are we going to legislate against them leaving? What choices do we have?' I replied: 'If the massive importation of cheap labour from China is politically not feasible, you have no choice but to let them go. Better this than to have them wiped out.'

A colleague asked, 'With all that cheap labour available, shouldn't capitalists be better off? Why are you predicting that advanced capitalist countries will face all kinds of problems?' My answer: 'Capitalists are going to do well—wealthy Japanese for example—but not in their own countries, not in those particular locations.'

The problem with the law of comparative advantage is that it ignores transaction costs. If factories in the suburbs of Osaka, for example, are moving out, or if they are not expanding, it would make no sense for these businesses to acquire big offices in downtown Osaka. They would rather acquire big offices in Hong Kong, where cheap labour is less than an hour away. This is not what the textbooks tell you. For American enterprises and Canadian enterprises moving down to Mexico or Latin America, it makes no sense to keep big offices in Chicago or Toronto. And that is the reason why Osaka's office values have dropped by as much as 80 per cent, while prime office space in downtown Chicago is now renting at only US$10 per square foot per year. The story in Toronto is even more dramatic: premium office space, now available at near-zero rent, may be bought at less than 80 per cent of construction cost.

It is certain, therefore, that we are going to see some fundamental structural changes the world over. The process will take at least twenty or thirty years to complete. There will be problems for high-wage countries with strong labour unions and big social welfare programmes. These countries may enjoy mild recoveries now and then, but their relative trend, no doubt about it, is down, down, down. It is difficult for me to see that politics will allow them to import cheap labour on a massive scale. It is difficult for me to believe the United States would cut social security tax—which now runs at 16.2 per cent—to 2 per cent, the level with which they began in 1937. With all sorts of social welfare programmes coming in and the minimum wage going up, the American economy is going to be hard hit, not at once, but gradually and surely over time. Basic manufacturing is in danger of going under.

Recently a friend of mine talked about emigrating to Canada, where you have to invest a certain sum to get resident status. He was going to open a factory, and I told him he needed his head examined. You've got to be crazy to think about going to Canada to manufacture garments. Miracles may happen but the odds are not in your favour.

Though wrong in detail, the factor–price equalization theorem is basically correct. It states that the international movement of goods and the international movement of factors of production are equivalent. Free trade in goods substitutes for free migration of labour. As a result, workers in high-wage countries are going to have problems because of the enormous availability of cheap labour.

It also follows that management-level people, financial people, people who arrange things and know how to borrow money for development and projects, are all going to be in a relatively good position for some time to come. Not a very long time though, because I think the Chinese are learning these skills, perhaps faster than we in Hong Kong would like. You know the story about Hong Kong people going into China to open restaurants and making a fortune a few years back? At first the Hong Kong managers and chefs all did very well income-wise. But now many of them have been fired and are coming back, because the Chinese have picked things up. They may not be able to cook as well as Hong Kong chefs, but they can do 80 per cent, and that is good enough.

Another implication follows from the marginal productivity theory: countries with lots of cheap labour or easy access to cheap labour will experience substantial rises in property values. That's right! I see many in the audience smiling with the property and stocks you are holding, and this is not without reason—marginal productivity theory tells us that if the price of labour goes down, property prices will rise in places where there is easy access to cheap labour.

Then there is a third result: given the demand for finance the world over, whether from Russia, China, India, Vietnam, or Mexico, the real rate of interest—the nominal rate of interest minus the rate of inflation (if you will allow me to be a little sloppy)—is going to stay high for some time to come. I think in real terms the rate of interest is going to be up there for ten to twenty years at least. Now some of you may ask: how can this be correct? Hong Kong's inflation is nearly at 10 per cent; the money rate of interest is so low that the real rate is negative. This is an interesting question, but it requires a long discussion. Briefly, the kind of 'inflation' people talk about in Hong Kong right now is not really inflation at all—not in Milton Friedman's sense. It is rather a reflection of sharply increasing productivity and wages, as a result of soaring demand for management and other Hong Kong services for China.

Because of Hong Kong's linked exchange rate, its interest rates are governed by those in the United States. People may then ask an even more difficult question: since real interest is going to be high, how come interest rates in the United States or Japan are so low? Inflation is low and interest rates are also low. Right now the interest rate in the United States is about 3 per cent and inflation is about 2 per cent, so we are talking about a 1 per cent real rate and that is not high. But this is not the answer. The answer is that, during the last several years, the yield curve in these countries has never been steeper. At least I myself do not recall a steeper yield curve. The long-term interest rate is higher than the short-term rate by more than twice. Right now, the long-term rate in the United States is over 7 per cent, as compared to a short-term rate of about 3 per cent. Moreover, there is no substantial revision of inflationary expectations in the United States right now. Inflation is expected to be low, but somehow the long-term rate refuses to fall. This reflects what I've been saying. The real long-term rate is high internationally: it has been high in the United States for several years, and also in Europe and Canada. I think it will continue to stay high. Over the next ten years at least, or perhaps for as long as thirty years, the real long-term rate should remain in the neighbourhood of 3 to 5 per cent. I would be surprised if it dropped below 2.5 per cent. A 2.5 per cent real rate is very high, because historically you would be looking at around 1 per cent.

This high real long-term rate shows what kind of demand the world is experiencing, for funds to finance long-term reconstruction and redevelopment. Not in the United States, where there is not much going on. However, if China demands more long loans, or Russia or Mexico do so, it will be reflected in the market, even in the United States, because banking and finance these days have become solidly international in nature.

So this is the global situation, in which there are going to be major, significant structural changes the world over. Managers and financial people will do relatively well. But countries with high labour cost and big social welfare programmes are going to have a hard time of it for twenty or thirty years to come. And the real long-term rate of interest will stay high, which compounds the difficulty of investing in advanced (high-wage and high-welfare) countries. Property values in cheap labour areas are going to pick up or stay firm.

Under the circumstances, if China continues as it has been—moving toward privatization on a massive scale and joining the international community—I can see nothing but bright prospects, very bright indeed, for Hong Kong. In this scenario, I think the Chinese economy is going to be fiercely competitive. I have been urging my Beijing friends over and over again to do away with trade barriers. Just open it all up. Then ask other countries to open up too. Should this happen, then it is a safe bet that the Chinese will gain immensely. Why worry about trade? Why worry about importing American cars? Import anything you want. Let everything in and abolish the customs office, and try to persuade the other side, the United States or whoever, to reciprocate. In a fair fight with free trade, my money is on China. In this case, Hong Kong people are going to make so much money, that every Chan, Lee, and Cheung will be beaming from one corner of their mouths to the other, because we are going to sit in the middle and take part in the buying and selling, and the financing. And why not? It is good for them, it is good for us, and good for our children. And it's good for Hong Kong University too: we would be sure to get a pay raise every year!

The scenario is attractive, but let's go on to something that is not so encouraging. My research on property rights has led me to conclude that there are fundamentally only three different kinds of rights systems in the world—not as many as I used to believe, or even my friends working on property rights still believe.

In the first kind, the rights of individuals are delineated in terms of property, in terms of the things one owns. This is the private-property system or the capitalist system. Li Ka-shing[2] can enjoy better housing and more goods and services than I can, simply because he owns more things than I do. People in Hong Kong are unequal because of this discrepancy in property rights, because the resources they command are unequal. Now you may not like it, and, for myself, I would prefer resources to be distributed according to years spent in university. But, under the private-property system, human rights are equal, and people are therefore equal before the law. It is possible to have a system of jurisprudence in which there is rule of law.

The second kind of system is communistic, as Mao envisaged. Everyone is supposed to be 'propertyless'. People are equal in terms of property because nobody has any. As a result, and as dictated by a theorem of mine expounded elsewhere, they become unequal in terms of human rights. Deng Xiaoping's son certainly possesses more rights and privileges than my son. Because human rights are not equal, people cannot be equal before the law. Consequently, it is pointless to suggest that a legal system like ours should be introduced into a communist system. Under communism people operate like an army: the rule of discipline prevails, but not law in the judicial sense. How can you have a judicial system when individuals are not equal before the law? You cannot.

---

[2] Li is a real-estate development tycoon and one of the richest men in Hong Kong.

This is what happens under communism: people's rights are not defined in terms of properties, but in terms of hierarchical ranking. It is not that individuals have no rights—they have lots of rights, they talk about rights all day long—but their rights are defined by how highly placed you are in the administration, how many years you have been in the party, and so on. Once I worked out a matrix representation of who outranks whom in China: it makes fascinating reading.

Finally, there's a third kind of system in which neither property rights nor hierarchical rankings are well defined. The rights to corruption, on the other hand, are defined by regulations. This is what I have called the 'India system'. One official is in charge of ladies' handbag imports, another is in charge of exchange control, and a third is in charge of men's watches. It is difficult to corrupt without regulations. In Panama, corruption rights are so well outlined that Official A makes it his business on Mondays, Tuesdays, and Wednesdays, and Official B on Thursdays, Fridays, and Saturdays, and it is all a part of the system.

Corruption is one thing, but if you are talking about an accepted right to corrupt it is another. When the right to corruption becomes as defined as in India, then it becomes a system. Once that has happened things become very difficult to improve. I mean, India has democracy, they vote every other day. They have done this for forty years and—you know what has happened—most of the country is starving. People talk about corruption all the time, complain about corruption all the time, but nothing changes. Things have degenerated into a situation in which corruption has become enshrined in a rights system.

When large-scale corruption emerged in China around 1984 and 1985, I was delighted because it was inevitable. Desirable economic reform in China is essentially a process of transforming the country from a system in which rights are defined in terms of hierarchical ranking to one in which they are defined in terms of property. There are many obstacles to this process. One of the most serious is that, in changing from one to the other, you have to go through the 'India system'. Under the original system, privileges follow from rank, but it is not corruption—I am the son of a high official, so I am entitled to hospital treatment before the fellows standing in line; if you want to jump the queue you must give me some benefits, because I have the right to do that.

However, corruption in transition is one thing, corruption as a well-defined rights system is another. The grave danger of the Chinese reform process is that it may get stuck in the middle and become another India!

Since I took up the Chair at the University of Hong Kong in 1982, I have been sitting on the edge of my chair during the day and having nightmares at night. All the time I was hoping that China would move from hierarchical ranking to private-property rights, without having to spend too much time in the middle. That's the part which I called the 'passage to India', and that is why, from early on, I have firmly held the view that gradualism in reform is undesirable.

From 1986 onwards, I have been shouting at the top of my voice on every occasion that China seemed in danger of being stuck in the middle. Every now and then the India syndrome would seem to take hold, but luckily for China big events would happen—shocks which would shake it loose. You may remember in 1987 the Chinese government, as part of its programme to reign in inflation, was talking about dividing different products into categories and drawing up pricing regulations for each. I said, 'My God, this is India!' In the process of doing so, they brought about the events of 4 June 1989. In my view, the June Fourth Incident was certainly sad, but it did help to stop this regulation-framing process. In effect, Beijing gave in to the local authorities and said, 'Look, do whatever you like, so long as you keep the people quiet and keep the students off the streets.' As a result the 'passage to India' was interrupted, which explains the spectacular growth the country experienced in 1991 and 1992.

If you look back at the Chinese economic development in the past fifteen years or so, 1991 and 1992 represent the two best-performing years. However, from 1993, I have started to take a more pessimistic view, for the first time since 1979. It all started about June 1993, with the renminbi falling sharply, inflation rising sharply, and Vice-Premier Zhu Rongji taking over as head of the People's Bank of China. Mr Zhu made some very encouraging statements, but by August, nothing had happened: it was all talk. This dawned on me when I again took Milton Friedman to China in October. And it became even clearer at the beginning of 1994, when China dropped its multi-tier exchange control, and brought in all those supplementary regulations which made things worse.

The three men now in charge in China, Li Peng (the Premier), Jiang Zimin (the President), and Zhu Rongji, are all engineers. They like to treat the country like engineers controlling a machine. But the problem with human beings, individuals in the market-place, is that they are not machines, and putting in a bolt here and tightening a screw there will not help. But that's what they are doing. When they see grain prices rising, they simply declare that all state enterprises should unite to control prices. When they talk about relaxing exchange control, they prevent outside currency being circulated in China. How can this work? There are billions of Hong Kong dollars inside China, and if you don't allow them to be circulated, and don't allow them to be moved back to Hong Kong, what can people do with them? Burn the stuff? It does not make sense. And then, you may recall, in 1993 Shenzhen announced it intended to reduce capital-gains tax from 40 per cent to 20 per cent, yet immediately afterwards Beijing announced that capital-gains tax would be sharply increased throughout the country. Shenzhen is part of China—so the right hand does not know what the left hand is doing.

I have been following events in China very closely since 1979. Every time I have seen a step backward I have not felt alarmed, because I know that this to-ing and fro-ing is inevitable. A backward step is often necessary to prepare for the next step forward, and, as long as the direction remains correct, it should be all right. But, from the end of 1993, I have seen no sense of direction at all. I don't know what the engineers are doing, or where things are going. I don't know what is happening with the People's Bank, for example, the exchange control and price control. There is no clear direction.

Deng Xiaoping is old and ill. Those of you who watched him on TV must have been shocked that day.[3] The man is old and China must have a strong man for at least a few more years. You cannot all of a sudden replace strong-man

---

[3] During the Chinese Lunar New Year holiday of 1994, Deng was shown on Hong Kong television watching a fireworks display.

rule with democracy, particularly since there is no well-defined constitution. So, who's going to be the next strong-man? I feel that everybody in China is waiting for something to happen. And in the meantime high-ranking comrades, their sons, and their daughters, go merrily on with their business of corruption. The right to corrupt is becoming more and more clearly defined. The resulting polarization in income distribution reminds me of the Guomindang period (1927 to 1949). China is heading towards the India system, and once it becomes firmly established, that will be that.

You may ask: what will happen to us if China becomes another India in five or ten years time? Well, Hong Kong will be another Bombay. It would be a wonderful place for the high comrade to keep a mistress and launder money. It wouldn't be too bad. Bombay is prosperous. I think Hong Kong people, smart as they are, will do well in the corruption game. But it would not be a place where you would like to raise your children. People here are already talking about connections in China, learning about loopholes. Many Hong Kong businessmen and Chinese princelings are already 'holding hands'. This is not a healthy development. Polarization of income will continue. And, as you look ahead, if China becomes another India, the Hong Kong partnership will be as strong as before, but it will be different. It is something I don't like to talk about, but it is a real possibility. I think the chance of it happening is more than 50:50, unless something drastic should happen in the next couple of years.

The great Sung poet Su Tung Po once said, 'We do not know the real picture of Lu Mountain, because we ourselves happen to be at the heart of it.'[4] We are approaching the new century, and in another hundred years or so, when we are gone, historians will look back at our place, our time, as if they are looking at Lu Mountain from afar. What will they say? Well, I think what they will say first is that the collapse of communism at the end of the twentieth century constitutes one of the great events in human history. The economic historian will say more. Because it all started in China,

---

[4] My translation. For another rendering of this verse, see Burton Watson (trans.), *Su Tung-P'o: Selections From A Sung Dynasty Poet*, New York: Columbia University Press, 1965, p. 101.

they will say that the hero of this great event is not Gorbachev, or Thatcher, or Reagan; they will say the hero is Deng Xiaoping. And I think historians will also say that Hong Kong, at long last, put itself on the map. We, its people, contributed mightily to the capitalistic movement in China, and, as a result, led the communist world to change in the same direction.

But there are two different ways in which these historians might conclude their chapters. One way is that China will move further towards private property, equal human rights, law and order, and Hong Kong's people will live happily ever after. With this the historians will predict that around the third decade of the twenty-first century, China will become the world's major economic force. On the other hand, historians may describe the ensuing corruption and the breakdown of law and order, implying the breakdown of civilization. Of course, Hong Kong people would still be doing pretty well living in a prosperous but decadent Bombay. But that will not be something historians would write about with great admiration.

Ladies and gentlemen, we are on the threshold of that development. We are at a critical time, in a critical place. We hope there may be something we can do to improve things, but we feel so helpless. We are little people who can do little, although we wish we could do more, but it is true that history is in our hands.

7 'One Country, Two Systems': An Idea on Trial

AMBROSE Y. C. KING

Time for an Account

ALMOST TEN years ago, the British and Chinese governments, out of a sense of historical inevitability, a sense of political realism, and as an act of will and imagination, reached an agreement on the future of Hong Kong. Today we all know this agreement as the Sino-British Joint Declaration. It embodies the spirit of 'one country, two systems': Deng Xiaoping's vision for Hong Kong and the reunified China after 1997.

Although there was no shortage of enthusiasm for the idea of 'one country, two systems', there was great doubt and pessimism regarding its implementation. Simply put, since the Joint Declaration was announced, the idea of 'one country, two systems' has been on trial. After seventeen rounds of talks on Hong Kong's political reform proposals, the communication between the two sovereign powers suffered a total 'breakdown'. On 23 February 1994, to quote *The Economist*, 'The divorce papers between China and Britain [were] filed.' As a result, *The Economist* wrote, 'So it is goodbye to "convergence", the idea of continuity of political development across the 1997 threshold, and it is, almost certainly, goodbye to the 'through train', the mechanism whereby those elected to Legco in 1995 could sit there until 1999.'[1]

But how about 'one country, two systems'? Neither Governor Patten, the mastermind behind Hong Kong's political reform proposals, nor the Chinese government have said goodbye to the concept. Mr Patten seems to take the view that his democracy project which is 'open, fair and acceptable to Hong Kong people' can only aid the realization of the 'one country, two systems' concept, which is already embodied in the

[1] *The Economist*, 5 March 1994, p. 30.

Basic Law of the Future Special Administration Region. China, on the other hand, warning in terse and unambiguous words, is prepared to set up a new 'stove' on 1 July 1997.

The idea of 'one country, two systems' is not yet dead, however. It will be on trial up to and well beyond 1997. What I plan to do in this paper is to give an account, as a reminder, of what the trial has entailed in the past ten years and to examine, briefly, how the concept of 'one country, two systems' looks for the future.

An Imaginative but Untested Concept

After two years of prolonged and strenuous talks starting in September 1982 the governments of the United Kingdom and the People's Republic of China signed the Joint Declaration on 26 September 1984. The main thrust of the Declaration is as follows:

> On 1 July 1997 the sovereignty of Hong Kong will be restored to China. Hong Kong shall became a Special Administrative Region (referred to hereafter as SAR) enjoying a high degree of autonomy. Hong Kong will continue to preserve its present form of capitalist system with executive, legislative and independent judicial power, including that of final adjudication for 50 years from 1997.

According to Deng's idea, Hong Kong would reintegrate with China in 1997, but would continue to have its own principles of governing and ways of life based on the capitalist system, whilst mainland China would continue its socialist system. The then British Prime Minister, Margaret Thatcher, considered 'one country, two systems' an imaginative concept, and her government recommended the Declaration to the people of Hong Kong with considerable enthusiasm. The Declaration was seen as the 'best possible deal' that Hong Kong people could reasonably hope for. From what we can gauge from editorials, comments, and reports in the press, as well as survey findings of independent research institutes, the overwhelming majority of the Hong Kong population were in favour of the Declaration, though most of them were not without reservations of one kind or another. The United

States and Japan, two of Hong Kong's major trading part-
ners, readily endorsed the agreement immediately after the
Declaration was announced. Also supportive were the European
Economic Community (EEC, now the European Union) and
other countries in Asia, with the notable exception of the
Republic of China in Taiwan.

Given the overriding normative principle (which no one
can possibly challenge) that colonialism should come to an
end, Britain had no grounds to fight against the return of
sovereignty to China, and no one in China including Deng
Xiaoping, who wanted or could afford to be another Li Hong
Zhang,[2] were willing to extend the British right to continue
to rule Hong Kong beyond 1997. Moreover, legally, politically, culturally, and physically, independence was an equally unfeasible alternative for Hong Kong. Therefore, a referendum
was never considered seriously as an option. Under such a
circumstance, the formula of 'one country, two systems' was
arguably an attractive, and indeed, imaginative solution to
the question of 1997. This was why, on the whole, the people of Hong Kong, who had been denied a say in the Sino-
British negotiations, accepted the British 'recommendation'
without too many misgivings.[3] It is worth mentioning that
notable democratic activists, including Martin Lee and Szeto
Wah, were appointed to the Basic Law Drafting Committee
in order to incorporate the idea of 'one country, two systems', and to write the mini-constitution for the future Special
Administrative Region (SAR). It can be fairly said that in 1984
there was a broad consensus among Hong Kong élites, both
within and without the government, that it was an enor-
mously difficult, but not impossible task, to transform the
idea of 'one country, two systems' into reality.

Notwithstanding the fact that 'one country, two systems'
commanded no small degree of support from the people, the
idea was still a novelty and, above all, an untested concept.
There was considerable suspicion concerning the capability,

[2] Li Hong Zhang was once the foreign minister of the Qing Dynasty. He
ceded Taiwan to Japan after the defeat of the Qing in the Sino–Japanese
War of 1894–5. This was seen as a betrayal.
[3] See Ambrose Y. C. King, 'The Hong Kong Talks and Hong Kong Politics',
in Jurgen Domes and Yu-ming Shaw (eds.), Hong Kong: *A Chinese and
International Concern*, Boulder: Westview Press, 1988, pp. 42–60.

if not the intention, of the Chinese government to carry out its 'one country, two systems' pledge. While still basking in the relatively euphoric atmosphere of the post-Joint Declaration honeymoon, a survey conducted by local scholars showed that only 22.3 per cent of the Hong Kong people believed the Chinese government would truly let 'Hong Kong people rule Hong Kong'.[4] The lack of confidence in Hong Kong's future was clearly demonstrated in the continuing migration to countries such as Australia, Canada, and the United States. This 'exodus fever' reached a peak following the earth-shaking events of the Tiananmen tragedy on 4 June 1989, roughly five years after the signing of the Joint Declaration. Indeed, the Tiananmen incident was a watershed in the political history of post-Declaration Hong Kong. The change in Hong Kong's political ecology in the next five years (1989 to 1994) cannot be fully understood without appreciating the impact of the Tiananmen tragedy on the people of Hong Kong.

Intensification of Politics and the Search for Democracy

True enough, Hong Kong had been predominantly an economic and administrative city before the question of 1997 was first raised. Hong Kong had long been a politically inactive and economically dynamic city, ruled and administered by a vast and efficient government bureaucracy. The colonial government never seriously thought of transplanting British or any other Western-type democracy into the colony. For decades, the Hong Kong government had consciously and deliberately created hundreds of consultative committees at various levels of the bureaucracy, through which the views and feelings of the industrial-business élites, professionals, and ordinary citizens were fed back into the administrative decision-making process. The Legislative and Executive Councils are, amongst others, two organs which serve as important mechanisms to co-opt the local Chinese socio-economic élites into government. Through the extensive

[4] Kuan Hsin-chi and Lau Siu-kai, 'The Civic Self in a Changing Polity: The Case of Hong Kong', in Kathleen Cheek-Milby and Miron Mushkat (eds.), *Hong Kong: The Challenge of Transformation*, Hong Kong: Centre of Asian Studies, The University of Hong Kong, 1989, pp. 91–115.

institutionalized process of consultation and absorption, Hong Kong has developed a unique political system. The continuing and timely absorption of potential political élites into the administration has made politics outside the government almost unnecessary. It was no accident that until the 1970s, Hong Kong had prominent business people, industrialists, and bureaucrats, but no politician of significant stature. I have called this phenomenon the 'administrative absorption of politics'. I have also argued that the administrative absorption of politics, a system of 'élite integration' could only work well in a society in which the level of politicalization was relatively low.[5]

However, once the 1997 issue appeared on the political horizon, politicalization at the societal level began to accelerate and intensify, especially in the middle stratum. Pressure groups and political activists emerged one after another. It should be pointed out that, even in the 1970s, there were already signs of a rising political consciousness among the people due to industrialization and other forms of social change. Nevertheless, the conspicuous rise of politically oriented individuals and groups, and, later, parties or semi-parties, were mainly precipitated by the Sino-British negotiations, the Basic Law-drafting process and, above all, by China's slogan 'Hong Kong people rule Hong Kong', which was most inviting to the politically awakened people in general, and to élites of political will and ambition in particular. The intensification of politics did not come solely from the 'demand' side of the political system, with more and more people demanding to take part in the political process. It also came from the 'supply' side of the political system as both the British government and the Chinese government provided structural venues for political mobilization and participation.[6]

For decades, there was only an economic market in Hong Kong in which the dynamism of economics was devoid of

[5] Ambrose Y. C. King, 'The Administrative Absorption of Politics in Hong Kong', *Asian Survey*, 15, 5 (1975), pp. 422–39.
[6] The most conspicuous structural venues provided by the Chinese government for political mobilization and participation in Hong Kong at this stage were through the cooptation of Hong Kong social-economic élites into the Basic Law Drafting Committee and the Basic Law Consultative Committee.

politics. But starting in 1984, a 'political market' opened up, superimposed on the economic one.[7] Surprisingly or not, in the post-Declaration period (1984 and thereafter) and during the Basic Law-drafting period (1985 to 1990), more and more business élites, capitalists, and professionals, participated in the expanding political market, and a growing number of professional politicians emerged in the process of the marketization of politics.

At this juncture, it is worth mentioning that the concept of 'Hong Kong people ruling Hong Kong' which is part of 'one country, two systems' is by no means a concept without ambiguity. Nevertheless, it is clearly understood that it should be neither *Ying-ren zhi Gang* (British people rule Hong Kong) nor *Jing-ren zhi Gang* (Beijing people rule Hong Kong). It is well known that the success of 'one country, two systems' depends on nothing other than the full realization of the slogan of 'Hong Kong people rule Hong Kong'. And, to implement this ideal fully, the most reasonable conclusion must be that those Hong Kong people who rule Hong Kong after 1997 should be democratically elected by the people of Hong Kong.

Strategies and Approaches towards 'Hong Kong People Rule Hong Kong'

Almost simultaneously, whilst the British government was beginning its negotiations with China on the future of Hong Kong, the Hong Kong government put forward an Administrative Development Plan with its explicit purpose being to bring grass-roots leaders into government administration, thus bridging the gap between the government and the people. The District Board election in 1982 which was unprecedented in the colony's history, should be conceived as a step, albeit a small one, towards political democratization. And it was certainly no coincidence that the Hong Kong government issued a Green Paper on 'The Further Development of Representative government in Hong Kong' on 18 July 1984, just about two months before the Joint Declaration was signed.

[7] Ambrose Y. C. King, The Politics of the Three Chinese Societies [in Chinese], Taipei: Commonwealth Publishing Co, Ltd, 1988, pp. 167–80.

A White Paper on the same topic was finally published on 21 November 1984, about two months after the signing of the Joint Declaration. The stated aim of the White Paper was 'to develop progressively a system of government, the authority for which is firmly rooted in Hong Kong, which is able to represent authoritatively the views of the people of Hong Kong.'[8]

Unquestionably, the White Paper of 1984 was an important political document indicating the intention of the British to start decolonization by developing a limited form of democracy in Hong Kong. Thinking retrospectively, this document was nothing but a timely echo of the spirit, if not the words, of the Joint Declaration which says that 'the government and legislature of the Special Administrative Region will be composed of local inhabitants. The chief executive will be selected by election or through consultations held locally and be appointed by the Central People's government . . . . The executive authorities will be required to act in accordance with the law and will be accountable to the legislature', and, most importantly, 'the legislature will be elected'.

The 1984 White Paper not only expanded the local district boards by adding members through direct election, but also provided for twenty-four indirectly elected members of the Legislative Council for the election in 1985, ten of whom would be elected by functional constituencies, such as finance, banking, industry, law associations, medical community, unions, and other professional organizations. Indeed, the Hong Kong government's political reform was cautious and moderate. It seemed to be inclined to adopt a gradual process toward democracy and made known that Hong Kong would not follow the Western type of adversary politics.

However, the Hong Kong government's political reform caught Beijing by surprise. The Chinese government was clearly in favour of maintaining the status quo. The present system was perceived by the Chinese in the north as time-honoured, responsible for Hong Kong's social stability and economic prosperity. They were keen to preserve the essen-

---

[8] The Hong Kong Government Information Service, *Hong Kong 1985: A Review of 1984*, Hong Kong: Government Printer, 1988, p. 42.

tial features of the present system, and believed that what needed to be changed were those 'colonial' components, such as appointment of the Governor by the Queen.[9] By the time the Hong Kong government's 1984 Green Paper on 'Further Development of Representative Government in Hong Kong' was released, there were signs that the Chinese government was extremely uneasy and suspicious about the motives behind the Paper. In fact, warnings, subtle or otherwise, were conveyed to the Hong Kong government as early as July 1984. Chi Pengfei, then the Director of China's Hong Kong and Macau Affairs Office, expressed the view that China was in favour of 'stability and prosperity', not 'prosperity plus reform'.[10] In August, Xu Jiatun, then the Director of the Hong Kong New China News Agency (NCNA),[11] publicly warned against any hasty change in the Hong Kong government structure before 1997.[12] On 19 October 1984, Chi Pengfei told Donald P. H. Liao, then Secretary for District Administrations, that Hong Kong's political reform must 'converge' with the future Basic Law, and he said, in no ambiguous terms, that Hong Kong's future political system should be stipulated only by the Basic Law.[13] At first, the Hong Kong government's determination for further development of a more representative system seemed undisturbed; it stated that, until 1997, it had the sole responsibility and right for Hong Kong affairs, including political reform. Then, on 21 November 1985 Xu Jiatun dumbfounded the people of Hong Kong by charging that 'some people are not observing the Joint Declaration'.[14] This was the first sign of a Sino-British rift since the signing of Declaration.

In this connection, it should be pointed out, that from the

---

[9] Kuan Hsin-chi and Lau Siu-kai, 'Hong Kong in Search of a Consensus', Occasional Paper, The Centre for Hong Kong Studies, The Chinese University of Hong Kong, November 1985, p. 23.

[10] See *Ming Pao Daily News*, 25 July 1985.

[11] The NCNA was the *de facto* representative of the Chinese government in Hong Kong.

[12] See *Ming Pao Daily News*, 6 August 1985.

[13] Ku Hsing-hui, 'Signs of Hope for the Political Reform Controversy', *Ching-Pao* (The Mirror), 103 (1986), pp. 6–10.

[14] 'Xu's Speech Jolts Hong Kong Optimism', *Asia Wall Street Journal*, 25 November 1985.

beginning, the Chinese government never fully trusted Britain. China believed that the Hong Kong government's development of representative government was a conspiracy of *Min-chu Kang-kung* (using democracy to resist communism), intended not to preserve the characteristics of capitalism, but to transform Hong Kong into a 'separate political entity'—a city-state of its own—thus perpetuating British influence after 1997. In a nutshell, China, rightly or wrongly, was convinced that the British-Hong Kong government and its alleged 'Chinese agents' had engaged in a conspiracy to develop a British version of 'Hong Kong people rule Hong Kong', leaving China with a *fait accompli* in 1997. Indeed, as this review shows, long before Christopher Patten's arrival in Hong Kong in 1992, the Chinese government was already in conflict with the British-Hong Kong government, regarding the implementation of 'one country, two systems'. It was now public knowledge that, in late 1985, the British-Hong Kong government retreated from its previous position on the 1984 White Paper in which a process was set for Hong Kong's democratization, with a further increase in elected (perhaps even directly elected) elements for the elections to be held in 1988.

In the Green Paper entitled 'The 1987 Review of Development in Representative government' released on 27 May 1987, the Hong Kong government no longer argued for the direct election of some members to Legco in 1988. Instead, direct elections were only listed as an option. And, not surprisingly, the British-Hong Kong authorities were criticized by democrats as lacking sincerity and commitment in their claim to develop a representative government in Hong Kong. In February 1989, the Hong Kong government issued another White Paper, 'The Development of Representative government: The Way Forward', which stressed 'prudent and gradual change'. In the 1989 White Paper, it promised that in 1991 at least ten out of fifty-six members of Legco would be directly elected. Moreover, it acknowledged the need for 'convergence' between Hong Kong's political development before 1997 and the future Basic Law. With hindsight, we know that the 1989 White Paper was prepared only after the British government had struck a 'secret deal' with the Chinese government—to which I shall return later in my paper.

The Basic Law Drafting Process and the Tiananmen Tragedy

In 1985, almost parallel to the Hong Kong government's work on the development of a more representative system in Hong Kong, the Chinese government started work on drafting the Basic Law. The Joint Declaration contains the following statement:

> ... that the Basic Law will stipulate that the socialist system and socialist policies practised in the rest of the People's Republic of China will not be extended to the Hong Kong SAR, and that Hong Kong's capitalist system and lifestyle will remain unchanged for 50 years after the establishment of the SAR.

This is, of course, a statement of what 'one country, two systems' is supposed to be. However, the Declaration is a political document: its political will and wishes have to be translated into a legal code—the Basic Law—under which the future Hong Kong SAR will be governed. As mentioned above, the Hong Kong people were denied by the Chinese government any role in the Sino-British talks, which, according to Beijing, were the business only of the two sovereign states. However, unlike the Sino-British talks, which were an external matter, the drafting of the Basic Law was purely an internal matter. There was every reason, therefore, for the Hong Kong people to have a say in the process of drafting the Basic Law. The people of Hong Kong were fully aware that taking part in this process was their only chance to air views on their own future. The Chinese leaders in Beijing were aware that Hong Kong people's confidence in and support for the Basic Law was and is essential to the success of Hong Kong as a Special Administration Region, as well as to the 'one country, two systems' policy of reunification. It is widely known that the supreme policy of reunification does not only apply to Hong Kong, but also to Taiwan, the Republic of China. Therefore, the Chinese government made an understandably enormous effort to demonstrate its eagerness to have the people of Hong Kong participate in the holy mission of drafting the Basic Law.[15]

[15] See Ambrose Y. C. King, 'The Hong Kong Talks and Hong Kong Politics', in Jurgen Domes and Yu-ming Shaw (eds.), *Hong Kong: A Chinese and International Concern*, London: Westview Press, 1988.

This process began in July 1985 with the establishment of the Basic Law Drafting Committee (BLDC) under the auspices of the National People's Congress. The Committee consisted of fifty-nine members, thirty-six appointed from the Mainland and twenty-three from Hong Kong. The twenty-three appointees from Hong Kong (with only a few exceptions) were either from the élites of Hong Kong's industry and business, or prominent personalities of various professions. Although they were not democratically elected, they commanded considerable respect among the populace of Hong Kong. Following the establishment of the Basic Law Drafting Committee, the NCNA in Hong Kong made a great effort in setting up the Basic Law Consultative Committee (BLCC), which had a membership of 180. BLCC, unlike the BLDC, was supposed to be a Hong Kong-wide non-official civic organization with full representation of Hong Kong people from all walks of life. There is no denying that amongst the members were individuals who had political visions or critical attitudes toward communist ideology and the status quo of Hong Kong. But the great majority of them represented the establishment interest and were pragmatic realists. Whilst having a strong interest in maintaining the capitalist system, they were unsympathetic, to say the least, to the values of liberal democracy. The Chinese government made no secret that it was opposed to direct elections in Hong Kong before 1997, and insisted that direct elections in 1988 would fail to 'converge' with the Basic Law being drafted by China for promulgation in 1990. The Chinese government's uncompromising distaste for rapid democratization in Hong Kong was clearly manifested in its endorsement of the so-called 'mainstream model' recommended by the BLDC in its first draft, released in November 1988.

This 'mainstream model', advocated by Louis Cha, an influential Hong Kong member of the BLDC, opposed the early introduction of direct elections for both the SAR legislature and its chief executive. In essence, the mainstream model postponed the introduction of a fully directly elected legislature for at least fifteen years after the founding of the SAR—that is, not until 2012. Despite vehement criticisms and attacks of the pro-democratic lobby and liberal intellectuals, the BLDC, in January 1989, adopted this model. The first round of the Basic Law drafting process could hardly be said to have helped China win the hearts and minds of the majority of the Hong Kong people. According to a public-opinion survey conducted by the Hong Kong General Chamber of Commerce in November, 1989, the 'mainstream model' received only 4.1 per cent support of the people surveyed.[16]

Whilst people in Hong Kong came to terms with this set-back, the Chinese student democratic movement erupted in Beijing in April 1989. Never before had the people in Hong Kong showed such intense concern for and interest in events in China. The Joint Declaration had certainly made them fully aware that their fate had become inseparable from that of the Mainland. As the democracy drama unfolded in Beijing it captivated the souls and hearts of the people of Hong Kong. On 21 May one million people, and on 28 May one and a half million people, solemnly and peacefully marched on Hong Kong Island, protesting the communist suppression of the well-intentioned democratic reform movement. These two unprecedented and gigantic collective actions almost changed overnight the image of Hong Kong people as politically indifferent and apathetic. Furthermore, they marked the turning point of the Hong Kong people's political consciousness. Then came the bloodshed of 4 June with its catastrophic impact on Hong Kong casting a vast and long shadow over people's confidence in their future. According to a poll conducted before the Tiananmen incident, more than 55 per cent of the people polled did not believe China would keep its 'one country, two systems' pledge.[17] A poll in October 1989, four months after the Tiananmen tragedy, revealed that some 70 per cent of the repondents did not believe that 'China will honour the Basic Law in guaranteeing individual rights and a separate economic system'.[18]

The British government was quick to acknowledge the existence of a crisis of confidence in Hong Kong. Apart from offering UK citizenship with a full right of abode to a limited number of the 3.25 million holders of British Dependent

---

[16] See the *South China Morning Post Hong Kong Review 1990*, p. 13.

[17] Figures from the Pre-Tiananmen Incident Poll are reported in Joseph Y. S. Cheng, 'The Post-1997 Government in Hong Kong', *Asian Survey*, 29 August 1989, p. 733.

[18] Findings of the October 1989 poll conducted by Inrasia are reported in the *South China Morning Post*, 31 October 1989, p. 1.

Territories Citizen passports, the British, together with the Hong Kong government, were prepared to speed up the pace of democratization before 1997 as a way of retaining the talents and expertise for the key institutions, government, and private sectors. It should be mentioned here that on 24 May 1989 members of the Executive and Legislative Councils decided to accelerate constitutional reform by suggesting what was labelled the 'OMELCO Consensus model'. This aimed at having one-third of Legco directly-elected in 1991, increasing to 50 per cent by 1995. More significantly, in October 1989, even the conservative big business élites—known as 'The Group of 89'—together with BLCC and BLDC members reached a compromise with the democratic group in producing what was called the '4:4:2' model. This model referred to the proportional distribution of directly elected (40 per cent), functional constituencies (40 per cent), and electoral college-originated (20 per cent) for the legislature from 1995–2001. Nevertheless, the post-Tiananmen Chinese government showed no sympathetic understanding for the democratic sentiments and aspirations of the people in Hong Kong, despite there being powerfully demonstrated in the spring and summer of 1989. The Chinese authorities became, instead, more suspicious and worried about Hong Kong turning into a 'counter-revolutionary, subversive base'. It seemed that the Chinese government was more convinced than ever that a fast pace of democratization could only be detrimental to the 'stability and prosperity' of Hong Kong. Clearly, the Chinese authorities were oblivious to the fundamental changes in the political ecology of Hong Kong which had begun in 1984 and intensified after the watershed of Tiananmen.

Hong Kong is no longer a purely economic city. It has become a city baptized by ever-growing politicization. The demand for democracy can no longer be easily confined, let alone, ignored. Indeed, it can well be argued that, if Hong Kong is to enjoy its stability, democratization of the system is no longer a luxury, but is now a necessity.[19] It is no exaggeration to say that the governability of the sunset colonial

[19] See Ambrose Y. C. King, 'The Hong Kong Talks and Hong Kong Politics', in Jurgen Domes and Yu-ming Shaw (eds.), *Hong Kong: A Chinese and International Concern*, Boulder and London: Westview Press, 1988, pp. 42–60, and Ambrose Y. C. King, 'The Administrative Absorption of Politics in Hong Kong', *Asian Survey*, 15,5 (1975), pp. 422–39.

government may become questionable during its remaining years if the demand for direct elections for Legco is totally unaccommodated. In light of this political context, Sir David Wilson, then Governor of Hong Kong, made an official visit to Beijing in January 1990. On the top of his agenda was his aim to convince Beijing to agree to a faster pace of democratization than envisaged in the Basic Law draft. It was later revealed that before Sir David's trip, Sir Percy Cradock, Personal Adviser to Prime Minister Thatcher, had made a secret trip to Beijing, and had struck a compromise deal with the Chinese government.[20] On 16 February 1990 the BLDC Plenum voted to accept the final draft, and thus concluded the five-year-long Basic Law-drafting process. In little more than a month's time, on 21 March 1990, the Hong Kong government, with full knowledge of the contents of the Basic Law on constitutional structure, announced the Hong Kong political reform. A 'convergence' between Hong Kong's pre-1997 political reform and the constitutional structure under the Basic Law provisions was at last successfully achieved. Under this 'convergence' deal, the 1991 Legco, which has fifty-seven members in total, will have eighteen directly elected members from geographic constituencies; and, in the 1995 election, the last British-conducted one, the total membership of Legco will increase from fifty-seven to sixty, and two more directly elected seats will be added. Under the Basic Law, the 1995 formula will remain in effect until 1999. That is to say that those elected to Legco in 1995 will be able to sit across the 1997 threshold.

The Chinese government and the British-Hong Kong government at that time should have taken some comfort, though hardly pride, in achieving a hard-won agreement on 'convergence' and the 'through train'. In broad measure, the Hong Kong community, depite serious misgivings regarding the Basic Law final draft, felt relieved that both the British-Hong Kong government and the future sovereign authority had reached a compromise on 'convergence'. Understandably, there was no shortage of severe critics who openly denounced the Sino-British bilateral 'secret deal' on 'convergence' as

---

[20] See Sir Percy Cradock, 'Tragedy for Hong Kong', the *Sunday Morning Post*, 5 December 1993, p. 10.

nothing but a 'British sellout' or 'London's betrayal'.[21] It is quite obvious that behind the criticisms of Britain was disappointment over China's conduct in drafting the Basic Law. In the view of a liberal-minded historian, 'the Basic Law drafting process has contributed directly and seriously to the crisis of confidence in the future of Hong Kong—a future that is fast becoming unsalvageable without an effective democratization process.'[22]

The Changing Political Ecology and Patten's New Political Reform

At the outset of my paper, I quoted *The Economist* on the 'breakdown' of talks between the British and the Chinese governments. In the words of that distinguished journal, 'it is goodbye to "convergence", goodbye to the "through train" '. What a twist of historical irony it is! After months of painstaking negotiation in reaching a hard-won compromise on 'convergence', the British-Hong Kong government and the Chinese government are now set firmly in different directions.

Governor Christopher Patten's policy speech of 7 October 1992 to Hong Kong's Legco on Hong Kong's constitutional reform marked a turning point in Hong Kong's political history. Patten's policy speech, both in tone and content, was arguably one of the most eloquent and inspiring speeches promoting democracy in Hong Kong that the Colony has heard since 1984. He did not challenge the widely cherished concept of 'convergence'. He said he would follow the Basic Law and not increase the number of directly elected seats in Legco beyond twenty in the 1995 election. However, Patten's two main proposals ingeniously exploit loopholes in the Basic Law to the maximum possible degree in order to bring considerable democracy to the pre-1997 political system. First, he proposed that the 'election committee', responsible for choosing ten of Legco's sixty seats in 1995, should be composed

[21] Hong Kong Legislative Council Debate, 28 February–1 March 1990; see especially the speech by Martin Lee.
[22] Ming K. Chan, 'Democracy Derailed: Realpolitik in the making of the Hong Kong Basic Law, 1985–1990', in Ming K. Chan and David J. Clark (eds.), *The Hong Kong Basic Law. Blueprint for 'Stability and Prosperity' under Chinese Sovereignty?*, Hong Kong: Hong Kong University Press, 1991, p. 31.

of directly elected members from the district boards. The present appointed seats would be abolished. Second, he proposed that nine new seats for 'functional constituencies' would be filled by giving a vote to everyone who worked in the industries they covered—a potential electorate of 2.5 million, not much smaller than Hong Kong's total electorate of 3.7 million. Mr Patten's public speech was an instantaneous success, and was enthusiastically embraced by democracy politicians. In a poll conducted a few days after Patten's speech was delivered, 73 per cent of respondents agreed with the Governor's constitutional reform, and 60 per cent said that Patten had gone far enough to meet aspirations for democracy in Hong Kong; 48.8 per cent believed that the Hong Kong government should proceed with Patten's proposal even if Beijing rejected it.[23]

The Chinese government was enraged by Patten's political reform proposals, and viewed them as a clever circumvention of the deal they thought they had made with Britain in February 1990. True enough, technically and legalistically, Mr Patten's nine new seats for nine functional constituencies would not break the Basic Law, but they would be democratic in all but name. The Chinese authorities felt double-crossed by the undeniable reversal of Britain's Hong Kong policy of the past decade, and their reaction was swift and uncompromising. In their eyes, Patten's constitutional package was a breach both of the Joint Declaration and of the Basic Law, though London's independent lawyers testified otherwise to the House of Commons Select Committee on Foreign Affairs. The Chinese authorities repeatedly pointed out that China's objection to Patten's proposal had nothing to do with the issue of whether democracy should be promoted in Hong Kong, but everything to do with whether international commitments should be honoured. As Patten's stance on democracy won the support of Australia, Canada, the United States, and the European parliament, China became even more convinced of her theory of a Western 'conspiracy', namely that Patten does not act alone, nor is he solely concerned with perpetuating British influence in Hong Kong after 1997. Instead, the policy is a well-coordinated western

[23] The *South China Morning Post*, 10 October 1992.

conspiracy to use Hong Kong as a base to press 'peaceful evolution' into China. Believing it or not, statesmen of international stature such as Lee Kuan Yew (Senior Minister of Singapore), have readily given credence to this conspiracy theory.

Mr Patten, who was genuinely surprised by China's strong reaction, sees this conspiracy theory as a 'bizarre' view of Britain's decolonization. He remained arrogantly undisturbed by China's criticisms and stream of verbal abuse and this has done him more good than harm. As a matter of fact, China's continued attacks on him have made him a champion for democracy and elevated him to a world-class politician, a status no Governor of Hong Kong has ever achieved.

Mr Patten, self-righteously or not, believed he was working fully in accordance with the spirit and letter of the Joint Declaration, and was working honestly to achieve the 'one country, two systems' goal. This lofty goal, he believes, Hong Kong and Britain could readily share. In essence, what he tried to accomplish is a limited but viable democracy of which a decently elected legislature was a vital part of the fabric. In his view, only with a credible, that is, a directly elected, legislature in place is there a chance of making the Executive-dominated government accountable to the public, thus making 'Hong Kong people ruling Hong Kong' a reality. But, what the Beijing government fears is that a legislature, enjoying too high a degree of autonomy, will inadvertently, if not deliberately, transform Hong Kong into a separate, independent political entity. So, the tension between the British-Hong Kong government and the Chinese government lies in their respective emphasis on the single concept of 'one country, two systems'. While China places high priority on integration, reunification, and, therefore on 'one country', the British-Hong Kong government stresses the necessity of autonomy, and thus of 'two systems'.

While the lack of a minimum level of trust between the two sovereign countries continues, each side's efforts towards their respective implementations of 'one country; two systems' are bound to be met with suspicions and hostilities. This is amply demonstrated in the separate versions published by Britain and China explaining the breakdown of their relationship after seventeen rounds of talks in Beijing last year. Britain is convinced that China wants a rigged election for a pliant legislature. Douglas Hurd (the British Foreign Secretary), in an introduction to Britain's version, wrote 'our proposals . . . would produce electoral arrangements which were fair, open and, in our judgement, acceptable to the people in Hong Kong. The Chinese side's proposals . . . would not. They proposed electoral arrangements which would have restricted choice and left the elections open to manipulation.' On the other side, China has an equally deep-rooted suspicion of Britain's motives in championing democracy in the twilight of its 150-year rule of Hong Kong.[24]

At this juncture, it is worth mentioning that Mr Patten who is labelled a 'one-issue Governor' seems to have single-mindedly immersed himself in institution-building for the implementation of his version of 'one country, two systems'. There is no question that he has forcefully taken up the task of building the Legislature into a credible, democratic institution. Nevertheless, Mr Patten, as a seasoned politician, does not work in a political vacuum. As I have said, Hong Kong had become a political city long before he assumed the Governorship in 1992. The political market has been widely developed since the signing of Joint Declaration in 1984. In the post-Tiananmen period, the people of Hong Kong have, in general, become more politically assertive. The Hong Kong government's legitimacy can no longer be based merely on its effective delivery of economic performance, nor can its governing authority be sustained successfully through cooperation with the Chinese government. In the 1991 election, the landslide victory of the liberal-oriented candidates was a testimony to the ascendency of the rising democratic aspiration of the populace. More significantly, the United Democrats of Hong Kong taking up eleven out of eighteen directly elected seats was a clear rebuttal to the Beijing government. It should not go unnoticed that by the time Patten became the twenty-eighth Governor of Hong Kong, Legco had already become a centre for party politics. Mr Patten, who has no government party to rely on, had to come to terms with the parties or individuals with a popular mandate. Fully aware of the new political ecology, Mr Patten

---

[24] *The Economist*, 5 March 1994, p. 30.

made a decisive break with the guiding principles of Lord Wilson's term as Governor. He restructured the Executive and Legislative Councils, creating an American type of system. The Executive Council was separated from Legco, but would be accountable to it. Patten's strategy for maintaining a 'strong, executive-led government' was to make a tacit alliance with the United Democrats and other directly elected parties, like Meeting Point, and independent liberals. Moreover, he used his prerogatives to appoint liberal-minded individuals into Legco as his natural allies. Mr Patten's impressive personality and image-building as a champion for democracy not only captivated the minds and hearts of the people in Hong Kong but also in no time captured Legco.

For the remaining years of colonial rule, the government's effective rule over Hong Kong will become more difficult to maintain. But if this involves a choice between courting the cooperation of Beijing and wooing the support of democratic forces with growing influence from within, Patten's has already made his choice. This seems to be the compelling reason why Mr Patten decided to make an all-out effort of championing democracy in the twilight of Britain's 150-year colonial rule. In short, Patten's push for democracy was a calculated manoeuvre to control the changing political situation and to fend off the 'lame duck' fate of the sunset colonial government.[25] In an article for the *Spectator* in London, Mr Patten wrote:

> We could have spent our last years of sovereignty defending the indefensible against every pro-democracy politician in Hong Kong and against criticism or cynical opinion at Westminster and world wide. Events between now and 1997 would have made life increasingly uncomfortable for a government which would have lost its authority.[26]

The Big Trial in 1997

Short of some miracle, there is little hope that Britain and China will resume talks, let alone reach an agreement on the

[25] See Tsang Yok-sing, 'Ignorance of China Marred Campaign', the *South China Morning Post*, 3 July 1993, Review 2.

[26] The *South China Morning Post*, 14 January 1994, p. 21.

issue of 'convergence' that is acceptable to Britain, China, and Hong Kong. Following his victory in Legco on the 'easy' part of the proposed reforms, Mr Patten has already put the 'hard' part to Legco. How Legco will react to the controversial parts of Patten's reforms remains to be seen. The Chinese government in the National People's Congress, made crystal clear that the three-tier elections of 1994/5 will be dismantled on midnight of 30 June 1997 and a new legislature will be formed according to the provisions of the Basic Law. Sir Percy Cradock, the architect of the 'convergence' compromise of 1990, said: 'no one should doubt they [the Chinese] will carry out that threat . . . the result will be that . . . the legislature will be replaced with a much less democratic assembly and democracy will have suffered a permanent setback'.[27] But Mr Patten thinks differently. In his interview with *Time* magazine, published on 14 March 1994, Patten was asked to respond to a statement that he will have a legislature that serves for only two and a half years. Mr Patten replied:

> We'll see. Are the Chinese saying that their first act of sovereignty will be to turf people out of the Legislative Council who are not placed there by an outgoing British sovereign power, but elected by the people of Hong Kong? That will be quite a thing to say to the world.[28]

No doubt, Mr Patten, or more accurately, the British-Hong Kong government, has made a calculated decision, betting on the odds that China will not implement her threat, for the sheer reason that it will cost China dearly. Patten wrote earlier this year: 'if we have a credible system, why should China want to remove from elective offices in 1997 men and women who will have been elected by their fellow citizens? This is hardly the best way of winning hearts and minds.'[29]

This argument, whatever merit it has, is hardly persuasive to the ears of the Chinese authorities. For China, the British government has committed an act of perfidy which is not to be tolerated. Moreover, in the eyes of the Chinese authorities, the three tier election of 1994/5 under Patten's proposals are nothing but a plot to perpetuate British influence

[27] The *South China Morning Post*, 5 December 1993, p. 10.
[28] *Time*, 14 March 1994, p. 18.
[29] The *South China Morning Post*, 14 January 1994, p. 21.

in Hong Kong beyond 1997. Therefore, they have to be abolished at whatever cost. In a way, what happened between Britain and China was as much a contest of will as a conflict of 'principle'. The scenario of the contest from now until 1997 can hardly be conjectured. It is a no-win situation for the Hong Kong people. Ten years after the signing of the Joint Declaration, we are still uncertain whether the imaginative idea of 'one country, two systems' will successfully be translated into reality.

The idea of 'one country, two systems' is, as it was ten years ago, still on trial.

8 The Mass Media and the
Open Society
LOUIS CHA

After 1997, will we or will we not be able to enjoy the way of life that we currently enjoy? This is a question frequently asked. It is a question of the greatest concern to the people of Hong Kong. What is this way of life that we enjoy, this quality of life that we value so highly, and do not wish to risk losing? This can perhaps be answered in one short sentence: it is the quality of a life lived in a place where people are free, and where society is ruled by law. Present-day Hong Kong is such a place. There is a more succinct term to denote such a society. We can call it an 'open' society. We might call it a 'free' society. But 'free' is too loose an adjective. There are so many different degrees of 'freedom'. Take China, for example. China is a much freer society today than it was in the fifties, and still more so than it was during the Cultural Revolution. But life in China is by no means as free as life in Hong Kong. On the other hand, Hong Kong is not really as free as it should be—at least not in political terms. The majority of the people are subjects of a foreign power, represented by a Governor who holds constitutionally dictatorial executive power. No one can call a colony a free country. Hong Kong is inhabited by a population, 98 per cent of whom are Chinese. It is a British colony, and has been so for over a century and a half. And yet, it is an open society.

I

'Open society' is a rather technical philosophical term. The terms 'open society' and 'closed society' were first used by the French philosopher Henri Bergson, but with meanings quite different from the current ones I am employing, which were later given to the terms by the eminent British philosopher Sir Karl Popper. According to Popper's definition, 'the closed society is characterized by the belief in magical taboos, while the open society is one in which men have learned to be to some extent critical of taboos and to base decisions on the authority of their own intelligence (after discussion)'.[1]

A closed society is politically arrested, or frozen. Every decision is made by a dictator or an oligarchy according to fixed tradition. That tradition is taboo: it cannot be challenged by the people. In an open society, on the other hand, people can be critical of any taboo, can discuss any important issue freely, and reach decisions on the basis of collective rational thinking. A closed society is petrified; an open society is continuously changing and developing.

The most striking contrast is that between Athens and Sparta in the period of the 5th century BC (a period contemporary with the transition between our own periods of the Spring and Autumn and Warring States). The Greek city-states, after several centuries of development, experienced an economic crisis caused by the imbalance between the growth in population and the relative lack of land. Athens solved this crisis by developing trade, agriculture, mining, and manufacturing, and it evolved a democratic political system. At the same time the arts flourished. Sparta, unlike Athens, met the economic pressures, not by modifying its institutions, but by resisting change. The Spartan government adopted the most conservative approach possible to the problem, instilling rigid social discipline and fossilizing the social structure. Society remained agricultural, and a commercial class was not allowed to develop. The use of silver or gold was forbidden, and only an iron currency was permitted (this is reminiscent of the way in which only a few years ago the Khmer Rouge burned all bank notes in Cambodia and forbade the use of money). Spartan society as a whole practised a strictly militarized egalitarianism, a crude form of communism. They avoided dressing differently from each other and they ate in the communal mess. Spartiates, who comprised the original Spartan warrior-class and alone had full rights as citizens, had no private property, they despised wealth and comfort, and subscribed to ideals very much like

---

[1] Karl Popper, *The Open Society and Its Enemies*, Vol. 1, London: Routledge and Kegan Paul, 1952, p. 202.

those of Mao Zedong's People's Communes. The Spartiate couple did not live together—immediately after their wedding night, the man returned to live with his companions in a male dormitory, and to eat in the communal mess. Laws were not allowed to be written down, but were inculcated in the minds of the Spartiates by rigorous training undergone by every boy and girl.

Two of the most important characteristics of an open society are overseas trade and overseas travel. Both of these activities provide a chance for contact with outsiders. In China, for more than two thousand years, governments have tried to suppress the merchant class and to forbid sea-faring.[2] From the time of Qin-shi-huang-di, down to the early Qing dynasty, there have been numerous imperial decrees to that effect. The Chinese emperors and their courts have consistently tried to maintain a closed society, and to resist change.

II

In modern times, resisting change has become harder and harder. It is no longer feasible for governments to forbid trade and communication with other countries, and, in addition to this, the growth of the mass media has created a powerful weapon to weaken the closed society. All totalitarian regimes without exception do their utmost to control the mass media, their aim being to maintain absolute rule.

China in its very early history knew the value of public opinion. In 841 BC the King of the Zhou dynasty forbade the people to talk freely or criticize the court. He appointed a group of Censors-General (high priests) to control such 'libels', and punished offenders by death. The people dared not talk in public: 'in the streets they just exchanged glances' (*dao-lu yi-mu*)—a famous saying still commonly used today. After a short period the nobles jointly expelled the tyrant king and replaced him with a collective leadership, headed by two of the most influential nobles, until the Crown Prince was

---

[2] For example, Emperor Wu of the Han Dynasty imposed new taxes on the copper cash held by the merchants, and introduced state monopolies on salt, iron, and wine. During the reign of Emperor Tai-zu, founder of the Ming Dynasty, coastal people were forbidden to go overseas, and private foreign trade was prohibited.

enthroned fourteen years later. A large number of similar say-
ings have been handed down in Chinese history, and have
become part of the treasure-house of collective Chinese political wisdom. Among them we find: 'To stop the flow of words
is more dangerous than to stop the flow of water in a river'
and 'The Sovereign hears the words of Heaven through listening to the words of the people'. It is a great tragedy that
so few of ancient China's rulers, indeed so few rulers throughout the history of the world, have been wise enough to pay
heed to such teachings.

In early times books and pamphlets constituted the written media. Qin-shi-huang-di's wholesale destruction of books
in 231 BC was a famous—I should say infamous—historical
event. It was re-enacted on a vaster scale 2,200 years later,
during the Cultural Revolution.

In Europe the record cannot be said to be any better. The
trial, conviction and execution of Socrates in 399 BC; the publication of the Roman Catholic 'Index' of prohibited books;
the Court of the Spanish Inquisition and the burning of
heretics at the stake; the executions of Joan of Arc in France
(1431) and of Thomas More in England (1535); the purge of
Galileo in Italy; the witch-hunts in Europe—these are but a
few familiar examples.

In the Qing dynasty there were countless 'Literary Inquisi-
tions'. The authorities executed hundreds of men of letters
simply because they were offended by the thoughts expressed
in a book, or even by a few lines in a single poem. I have
described one such purge in detail in my novel, *The Deer and
the Cauldron*.

We need not discuss here the means used by modern
authoritarian regimes to censor and control the mass media.
George Orwell, in his novel *Nineteen Eighty-Four*, gives a vivid
description of how the tyrannical Big Brother succeeds in
achieving this end. This was not purely the novelist's imagination, but was drawn in large part from his study of the
actual practices of the ruling party in the Soviet Union.

III

After the book came the newspaper. In ancient Rome there
was a daily gazette called *Acta Diurna* (Daily Events), dating

from 59 BC. Its origin is sometimes attributed to Julius Caesar. Handwritten copies of this gazette were posted in prominent places in Rome (such as the Forum), and despatched throughout the provinces, disseminating official information to the populace. The Chinese authorities published their official government gazette for nearly one thousand, three hundred years (from 618–1911), longer than any other comparable official publication in the world. It contained exclusively such items as official court information, public appointments, proclamations, and edicts. Of course, in this instance, there was no need of censorship. The word used for gazette, *pao*, is, incidentally, still used today by every Chinese newspaper throughout the world.

The modern newspaper began with the commercial newsletters that circulated in continental Europe, reporting information on the availability and prices of various goods and services. These also included a certain amount of political news. At first sporadic, they gradually began to be issued on a more regular basis. These more frequent journals were always liable to suppression and subject to censorship and licensing. Subsequently direct censorship was abandoned, but attempts at control continued through taxation, bribery, and prosecution.

In 1712 the British Parliament imposed a tax on newspapers (one of the so-called 'taxes on knowledge'), aimed at curbing the nascent power of the press. The rate of duty was one penny for a whole sheet, which effectively doubled the price, killing the popular *Spectator* along with other newspapers. Government censorship was continuously practised under the guise of frequent prosecutions for libel. In 1810 the political essayist William Cobbett was imprisoned and fined for denouncing the practice of flogging in the army. But, gradually, through the efforts of prominent people and newspapers, especially the London *Times*, the principle of free press was established. The tax on newspapers was abolished in 1855.

The First Amendment to the Constitution of the United States contains the following words: 'Congress shall make no law respecting an establishment of religion, or prohibiting the free exercise thereof: or abridging the freedom of speech, or of the press; or the right of the people peaceably to assemble, and to petition the government for a redress of grievances.'

This is the basis of the commonly held modern concepts of freedom of speech and freedom of the press—freedoms which are now written into the constitution of almost every nation of the world. Unfortunately, the actual interpretation and implementation of these freedoms often fall far short of their original, true meaning.

IV

Freedom of speech and freedom of the press concern the relations between the citizens of a country and their states and governments. There are sometimes misunderstandings in this regard. A newspaper, for example, can refuse to publish a reader's open letter. But this reader cannot as a consequence accuse the newspaper of having infringed on his freedom of speech, or of having acted contrary to freedom of the press. Likewise a company employee cannot accuse his manager of restricting his freedom of speech just because that manager denies him the use of the company telephone for private conversations during office hours. Even a government can impose certain justifiable restrictions. The most famous example is the ban on shouting 'Fire!' in a theatre when a performance is taking place and the auditorium is full of people. Nearly all countries have laws controlling television and radio, though not necessarily newspapers— this is certainly the case in the United Kingdom, the United States, and Hong Kong.

It must also be said that sometimes reporters and editors working in the mass media exercise too much power, to the point where they themselves can be considered to be interfering with freedom of speech. This is especially true of the editor, who has the final say about whether any particular item of news is used or not. Everyone has prejudices and fixed ideas about most subjects. So-called 'unbiased opinion' is just an illusion. But in most open societies (and Hong Kong is one of them) no one can hope to control all of the mass media. The government cannot achieve this control, nor can the press magnates, simply because there are too many elements involved, too great a variety of media.

In Hong Kong we have over sixty newspapers and 400 magazines.

In this particular respect, Hong Kong can claim a greater degree of freedom of the press than in most other developed countries. With the exception of London, and a few other metropolitan cities, few places have so many newspapers representing such a wide variety of political points of view, and catering to such a wide spectrum within the community. No single element of the Hong Kong media can afford to withhold a particular item of news, or deliberately distort a fact: if it does so it will find itself challenged by its competitors and by the community. A well-educated and well-informed community will not allow itself to be cheated and maliciously misled for long. That is the essential merit of the open society, and the media have a role in helping to create, promote, and preserve this quality of openness.

In an open society readers have freedom of choice. They can choose freely from amongst the available media, and find the source of information that they consider to be most reliable and most interesting. To survive in this highly competitive market, the media must have the support of their readership. If they are habitually dishonest they will lose that support, and then they will die, or at least cease to be profitable. And in Hong Kong, with the exception of a few political propaganda organs, most of the existing media are profitable, or are going to become profitable, or hope to become profitable.

In other words, ethical journalism is dictated in Hong Kong, not only by a moral imperative, but by the very realities of the market. The market imposes a discipline of its own. In general, dishonest reporting and sensationalism are kept within tolerable limits. This is the principle of self-restraint, or, as it is sometimes called, 'self-censorship'.

V

Quite a strong accusing voice has been levelled against the Hong Kong mass media in recent years, claiming that they are learning to practise self-censorship in preparation for 1997. For some elements in the Hong Kong media that may be the case, but it is surely not true for the majority. It is true that the Hong Kong media are politer towards mainland China than they used to be; they do not criticize the communist authorities as severely as they once did. But I think the main reason for this is not their fear of 1997 approaching, so much as the fact that China itself is now adopting a policy of 'Reform and Openness'.[3] China itself is a more tolerant, and a more rational place; living standards are greatly improved there, and will improve further. But at the same time, the Hong Kong media continue to report many of the mistakes and blunders committed by both the central and provincial authorities.

A striking example of this was the response of the Hong Kong media to the Tiananmen Incident in 1989. They all, without exception, reported and condemned the military action taken by the Beijing government against the students and other citizens involved. And yet that was only eight years away from 1997. We should remember the courage of the Hong Kong media (including certain of the official communist newspapers) during the June Fourth tragedy of 1989.

Japan is generally recognized as the Asian country with the greatest freedom of the press. It seems appropriate to compare Japan with Hong Kong, since both are Asian societies with strong oriental cultural heritages. In his recent book, *Politics and the News Media in Japan*, Professor Ofer Feldman has written:

> Its [the Japanese press's] self-restraint in reporting is motivated partly by concern for human lives and partly by what it views as the national interest. One example of restraint, or self-imposed limitations, is voluntary censorship in reporting kidnappings. Even when police authorities keep the press fully informed of developments regarding such criminal activities, usually the press will not report any detail that could endanger the life of the victim until after the case is solved. Another example of restraint concerns the attitude the Japanese press shows toward China. In support of the Japanese government's effort to establish and maintain good relations with the People's Republic of China, the press has tended to avoid any criticism of China since the beginning of the 1970s.[4]

[3] This policy was introduced by Deng Xiaoping at the end of the 1970s.
[4] Ofer Feldman, *Politics and News Media in Japan*, Ann Arbor: University of Michigan Press, 1993, pp. 14–15.

Hong Kong journalists would doubtless exercise a similar self-restraint with regard to kidnapping. But we do not for one moment feel bound by considerations of China's, or any other country's, national interest.

For journalists, self-restraint and responsibility are always extremely important considerations. We all believe that news reporting should convey facts accurately and faithfully; that the personal opinion or taste of the reporter must not be allowed to colour his reporting; that one should guard against the possibility of news being used for propaganda purposes; and that although editorial comment is free, it should never knowingly depart from the truth. I myself, during my thirty-four years as Chairman of the *Ming Pao Daily News*, continually asked my staff in the editorial department to remember this motto: 'Comment is free but the facts are sacred'. For many years we printed this motto on *Ming Pao*'s 'Free Forum' page. It was originally coined by the great British journalist Charles Prestwich Scott, former editor of the *Manchester Guardian*, one of the world's most respected newspapers. He edited that newspaper for fifty-seven years, ten years longer than the span of my own journalistic career.

Very few governments refrain completely from trying to influence the media. We can only say that the more developed a country is, the less its media are subjected to control. In a survey of over fifty-eight countries, Japan was included in a list of twelve countries with the least tendency to control the press.[5] But even in Japan, the government has a certain interest in influencing the media. Taxation in Japan, when compared with Hong Kong, is quite heavy. But Japanese newspapers and private television networks are exempted from the payment of regular corporate taxes, whereas in Hong Kong a network such as TVB, or a newspaper such as the *Ming Pao Daily News*, pays millions of dollars in such taxes annually.

VI

The great Athenian statesman Pericles was a contemporary of Confucius. When Confucius died Pericles was about sixteen years old. Forty-eight years later, in 431 BC, Pericles

---

[5] J. C. Merril, 'Inclinations of Nations to Control the Press and Attitudes on Professionalization', *Journalism Quarterly*, Vol. 65, 1988.

delivered his famous Funeral Oration for those Athenians who had died in the first year of the Peloponnesian War against Sparta and her allies. A few sentences of this oration are worth quoting:

> The freedom we enjoy extends also to ordinary life: we are not suspicious of one another, and do not criticize our neighbour if he chooses to go his own way . . . . But this freedom does not make us lawless . . . . Our city is thrown open to the world; we never expel a foreigner . . . . We are free to live exactly as we please, and yet we are always ready to face any danger . . . . To admit one's poverty is no disgrace with us: but we consider it disgraceful not to make an effort to avoid it. An Athenian citizen does not neglect public affairs when attending to his private business . . . . We consider a man who takes no interest in the state not as harmless, but as useless; and although only a few may originate a policy, we are all able to judge it. We do not look upon discussion as a stumbling-block in the way of political action, but as an indispensable preliminary to acting wisely.

These words were uttered more than two thousand four hundred years ago; but they have a significant bearing on our discussion of the mass media and the open society today.

George Washington in his Farewell Address of 1796 called for both public enlightenment and self-restraint. These qualities, I believe, should be commended to all those practising in the mass media today.

An open society is not created in just a few years. Its evolution entails a constant process of change and development. And sometimes there are periods of retreat. The Athens of Pericles was an open society, but it was an open society with a large number of slaves. It goes without saying that the human rights of those slaves were totally neglected. Every society has its limitations, its own historical background, its own cultural heritage. We cannot use our own yardstick to evaluate another country's internal affairs. An open society tolerates individualistic expression; it does not suppress unorthodox thinking. It allows the free public discussion of any issue. An open society is continuously encouraging change for the better, and creating new opportunities for progress and development. Freedom for the mass media is one essential part of that society. If nothing new ever happened in a society, if there was no news, what would be the use of the news media?

VII

For over one hundred and fifty years Hong Kong has had no democratic political structure. But we have always had a free and influential press. The press, to a certain extent, performs the role of expressing public opinion, and it exercises a certain surveillance over the activities of the government. Public opinion is fully reflected in the press, and the Hong Kong government has generally paid heed to public opinion, especially since the disturbances of 1967. In comparison with other democratic countries, which have popularly elected representative parliaments, the free press in Hong Kong may exert a more significant influence on local political life.

Which brings us to the crucial question: After 1997, will there still be freedom for the mass media in Hong Kong?

The Basic Law of the Special Administrative Region of Hong Kong, Article 27, runs as follows: 'Hong Kong residents shall have freedom of speech, of the press and of publication; freedom of association, of assembly, of procession, and of demonstration; and the right and freedom to form and join trade unions, and to strike.' The Sino-British Joint Declaration, Annex I, Article XIII, states that 'the Hong Kong Special Administrative Region government shall maintain the rights and freedoms as provided for by the laws previously in force in Hong Kong, including freedom of the person, of speech, of the press, of assembly.' It enumerates scores of rights and freedoms—freedom of speech and of the press are ranked second, after freedom of the person (the right not to be unlawfully arrested or detained)—but articles and annexes and other such provisions in official documents are not necessarily effective guarantees. Many residents of Hong Kong lack confidence in these promises, however beautiful they may sound.

My own personal view is generally optimistic. But I have certain reservations. After 1997 I think that the Hong Kong media may well experience less freedom than they enjoy now. I do not envisage that the local authorities, or even the central authorities in Beijing, will openly control or censor the press. But I do see a heavier form of pressure looming ominously in the future. This subtle, but none the less powerful, form of pressure I would call 'influence' rather than 'control'. To deal with this influence needs a range of qualities and abilities: high standards of journalistic experience, a knowledge of Chinese history, an understanding of the past and of the mentality of the communists, and a skilful and diplomatic attitude. Hong Kong's journalists have these qualities and abilities, of that I have no doubt.

China is undergoing far-reaching and rapid changes. It is becoming a more open society. This entitles us to see the future for the Hong Kong media in a rosier light. China's rigid and dull journalistic style will surely not invade Hong Kong after 1997. It will rather be Hong Kong's lively, colourful and multi-faceted style that will move into China. In fact this process is already under way; it has not needed to wait for 1997. Recent statistics indicate that there are now over 1600 newspapers in mainland China, a spectacular growth since 1978. Quite a substantial percentage of these are semi-official tabloids and daily trade journals. Their contents are varied and lively. Besides the newspapers there are over 6,500 magazines of various kinds, devoted to such subjects as literature, art, culture, education, economics, and finance. An ongoing reform of the press is taking place in China, one that deliberately avoids publicity.

Life is full of the unexpected. But I have full confidence in the Chinese cultural heritage, in the extraordinary Chinese talent for dealing with difficulties and triumphing over extremities. As Pericles said, 'We are free to live exactly as we please, and yet we are always ready to face any danger. We love beauty without indulging in fancies, and although we try to improve our intellect, this does not weaken our will.'

Let us both hope and strive for the best.

9 The Transition and Unexpected Changes

LEUNG CHUN-YING

Today is the 26 March 1994. In less than three and a half years from now, China will resume the exercise of sovereignty over Hong Kong.

Since the initialling of the Joint Declaration in September 1984, Hong Kong has proceeded three-quarters of the way down the road of transition.

Today, the Hang Seng Index hovers around the 10,000 mark, ten times the monthly average of 1984. Prices of apartments in sought-after locations have reached HK$10,000 per square foot, again about ten times the level of 1984. Office rents, despite massive supply, are challenging Tokyo's to become the world's highest.

These facts provide a stark contrast to a rather dark but popular joke on the Hong Kong cocktail circuit in 1984: it was said that a notice was soon to go up in Kai Tak Airport asking the last person to leave Hong Kong to please switch off the lights. Of course, ten years ago, few people had the faintest idea that air traffic, both in and out of Hong Kong, would increase so much as to warrant, not just a new airport, but also a whole set of supporting infrastructure. Even fewer people would have ventured to suggest that one in seven of the passengers using the airport in 1993—four years before the overworked backdrop of 1997—would be bound for mainland China.

A local developer, not listed in, or 'delisted' from the local stock exchange, who has no foreign domicile, and who is wholly owned by one family, recently announced plans to build in Hong Kong the tallest building in the world.[1] The Occupation Permit for this massive structure will, when it is completed, carry the seal of the Hong Kong Special Administration Region government.

[1] The Nina Tower is currently under construction.

Legalistically the transition began in 1985 when the Joint Declaration was ratified. Practically, Hong Kong people have been preparing for the inevitability of 1997 from the day when Margaret Thatcher met Deng Xiaoping in September 1982. Whatever the commencement, history will record that the transition so far, despite countless wranglings between the Chinese and British governments, has been much smoother than expected. Similarly, few would argue that, during the transition period so far, the general quality of life for the average Hong Kong resident has not improved beyond original expectations.

It is therefore useful to examine the factors which have more than answered Hong Kong people's prayers. It is useful, not just because it satisfies intellectual curiosity, but for two other purposes.

First, a sense of the achievements so far by the three key parties—the Chinese and British governments and the Hong Kong people—will build a healthy base for more confidence and trust in tackling future issues. Each side has spent too much time bemoaning shortfalls rather than noticing accomplishments.

Second, an examination of this sort could be of practical value in charting the way forward, not just to 1997, but beyond.

The fact that Hong Kong has, to all intents and purposes, surpassed the most optimistic projections, is due to one factor: change.

Since the beginning of the Sino-British negotiations in 1982, Hong Kong people and international observers have concentrated on ways and means, guarantees and proclamations, to preserve the system and the way of life. The main text of the Joint Declaration, for example, carries a list of the basic policies of the Chinese government: in these twelve short paragraphs the words 'remain' are used three times, 'retain' twice, and 'continue' and 'maintain' once each. Such concentration on preserving the status quo, virtually to the exclusion of other considerations, was meant to address the crux of Hong Kong people's apprehensions: their fear of change, and of the uncertainties that such changes might bring. Many of their worries concerned rather mundane issues —passports, currency (and its international convertibility), the education system, language, international movements, and even ballroom-dancing and horse-racing!

Despite the wish for no change, Hong Kong has undergone a transformation. Some changes are by design, others by default, and most in ways that were not anticipated. Some of the developments are welcomed by some more than others. China also has changed, as has the interface between Hong Kong and the Mainland.

Surprisingly, and with the usual twist of irony that history is full of, it is the net effect of these changes, with the good neutralizing the bad, that has given Hong Kong a much better chance of stability and prosperity after 1997, before the 'no change' guarantees can be tested. These developments are subtle, gradual, and continual, and are totally independent of sovereignty considerations. Their cause and effect are no more apparent than the occasional media report on isolated events that the media industry considers newsworthy. Yet they are already part of everyday life in Hong Kong.

One of the early concerns on the part of the Hong Kong people was the lack of political figures, let alone political leadership, to fill the voids left behind by the British administration. The root of this concern lay in Hong Kong's apolitical tradition, and in the belief that everybody who is anybody had a more decent, meaningful and rewarding job than being a politician—which goes to show the distaste Hong Kong people had at the time for politics!

One of the attempted responses to this concern was to appoint the Vice-Chancellor of one of our universities to the head of the post-1997 administration. Proponents of this solution suggested that universities could, at times, be rather 'political' (there being not much difference between small 'p' and capital 'P') and a vice-chancellor could easily switch from administrating academic prima donnas to unacademic prima donnas.

Both problem seekers and problem solvers on this issue were not to know that before the 1980s ended, the Hong Kong political bandwagons would already be overflowing with drivers and passengers. Nor did they see the prospect in the early 1990s of these bandwagons publicly displaying signs of political parties—a description that was considered to be the ultimate taboo. Hong Kong was equally ignorant of the fact that before any of the vice-chancellors became politicians, the reverse had happened, again by default more than by design. A politician had become the Governor of Hong Kong, and therefore the Chancellor of Hong Kong's universities.

The arrival of a politician at Government House, together with new politicians in the Legislative Council, the municipal councils, the district boards, and all other advisory bodies, has changed the governance of Hong Kong beyond recognition. While the public remains largely apathetic, sometimes even cynical, and shows signs of fatigue—as is demonstrated time and again by the low voter turnout levels—the decision-making path in government has taken different, sometimes uncharted directions. Efficiency has been lost, and few would argue that the quality of administration has improved.

Despite the fact that the majority of the Hong Kong population still prefers not to register as voters, or having registered, not to vote, the general trend is moving away from the appointment and selection system in favour of elections and to a broader electorate base. This change in attitude, and the speed with which the change has taken place, again was not expected in 1984. The provision in the Joint Declaration, for the Chief Executive of the SAR government to be selected by election or consultation, did not meet with any objection. A couple of years later, demand for universal franchise and direct elections surfaced and quickly gathered momentum. The Joint Declaration has not changed, but the minds of many of the Hong Kong people have.

In a similar vein, the Basic Law provides for election to half of the sixty seats in the first SAR Legislative Council by functional constituencies. This method was proposed by the Hong Kong government in the 1984 Green Paper and has been in use since 1985. The change in the definition and composition of functional constituencies by the Hong Kong government nine years after they were first introduced, also by the Hong Kong government, was totally unexpected. The Basic Law did not change, the minds of the Hong Kong government did.

When the subject of Hong Kong's future was first mooted in the late 1970s, some commentators believed that, since China was recovering from extreme political dogma, British administration of the colony might be allowed to continue beyond 1997. On this premise, various formulae were offered. It was suggested that perhaps China would consider resuming sovereignty over the ceded parts of Hong Kong in exchange for extending British administration. The different variations on this theme included discussion of whether a monetary reward might be offered to China to sweeten the deal. Others preferred to leave the whole issue open-ended by giving China the right to repossess Hong Kong by serving on the British a fifteen-year notice.

China's position on the future of Hong Kong became public in September 1982, but her determination was not accepted until April 1984. Even then, there was a considerable body of opinion expressing reservations about, or outright objections to, the concepts of 'one country, two systems' and 'Hong Kong people ruling Hong Kong'. To many people, China's determination was a departure, a totally unexpected change, from her earlier soothing words, asking investors to put their minds at ease. The very fact that China did not enter into such deals was a surprise for many.

To China, applying the idea of 'one country, two systems' to Hong Kong was perhaps equally unexpected. The first public document that gave the concept an airing was the 'Message from the Standing Committee of the Fifth National People's Congress to Taiwan Compatriots on New Year's Day 1979', nearly four years before Margaret Thatcher raised the issue of Hong Kong with Deng Xiaoping. China's policy to resolve the issue of Hong Kong's future was founded on 'appropriate' timing. With the benefit of hindsight, the British government and Hong Kong investors probably were inappropriately impatient.

Faced with uncertainties over 1997, the question of Hong Kong people's nationalities, and the meanings of these nationalities, quickly came into focus. On the subject of British nationality, it was not so much that the change first mooted in the 1977 Nationality Green Paper, was unexpected, but the need in the minds of many Hong Kong people for a foreign nationality or a foreign passport as a result of the Sino-British talks was surprising. By then, the doors had already been firmly closed on Hong Kong holders of what were purported to be British passports.

Reality as usual was quickly accepted. The lobbying and appeals receded. However, the twists and turns of Chinese history led to the events of 4 June 1989 which many consider to be the watershed in Hong Kong's transition. In the aftermath of the June Fourth Incident, the subject of nationality was reopened. The Hong Kong people again changed their minds and the British government had to revise, albeit partially, its well entrenched policy and give full British nationality to the selected.

The June Fourth Incident in the context of 'one country, two systems'—the cornerstone of confidence building—came as a rude shock, not only to Hong Kong, but also, possibly more so, to the Chinese leadership. Previously, in order to support the enshrining of a greater degree of autonomy in the Basic Law, Hong Kong people pointed to the 'two systems' part of the concept, emphasizing that the Hong Kong system, being different from that on the Mainland, should not be sacrificed for the 'one country' part, and should as far as possible be kept intact. Mainland officials and some Basic Law Drafting Committee members countered by emphasizing the fact that, while Hong Kong would have a different system, it would only do so as part of China where all the sovereign rights and responsibilities were to be vested in the central government.

Hong Kong responded enthusiastically to demonstrations by students and others in Beijing in May 1989, and was mobilized to a scale that Hong Kong had never before experienced. Donations were sent to the demonstrators, and petitions were sent to the Chinese government on their behalf. The handling of the demonstrations by the Chinese government also drew violent reactions from Hong Kong, culminating in some demands made publicly to overthrow the Chinese leadership, to boycott Chinese state-owned enterprises in Hong Kong, and for foreign governments to impose sanctions on China. Hong Kong, for right or wrong reasons, played a much more active role than Taiwan or Macau.

The reactions in Hong Kong were not expected, but were natural. After all, Hong Kong is part of China and 98 per cent of the population are part of the Chinese people. 'Blood is thicker than Water', as the slogan on many banners flying over Hong Kong said.

The Chinese government was quick to regurgitate the same

argument that Hong Kong itself had previously used often: that mainland China has its own system, different from Hong Kong's, and that the two systems should not seek to interfere with one another. Whatever the relationship between blood and water, well water does not mix with river water.

The Tiananmen incident was the first test of the 'one country, two systems' concept. It came as a revelation to both sides that, after all, there was some merit, under certain circumstances past, present, and future, in the other side's arguments. And both sides have been quick, unexpectedly so, to switch to these arguments as events unfold. The concept, with its inherent contradictions, has remained in fine balance.

Since the early days of Hong Kong, the ebbs and flows of Hong Kong's future have been linked to those of the Mainland. The announcement of China's intention in 1982 to resume sovereignty over Hong Kong by 1997 brought this relationship into sharper focus. This sharp focus contained two superimposed images: on the one hand, mainland China, the Chinese government, and its policies as of 1982, and, on the other, Hong Kong being subsumed into China in 1997. This rather grey montage, then, became a still picture, incapable of adjusting to some of the greatest and most encouraging changes that China, her successive governments, and her people have ever witnessed.

Given the crucial relationship between the Mainland and Hong Kong, it is indeed surprising that the Hong Kong government, together with local opinion shakers and movers, could be so insensitive to the latest developments across the Lo Wu bridge. Hong Kong maintains representations in many overseas countries, under different descriptions and with different briefs, except in mainland China. Hong Kong has no listening posts, no instant contact points and no lobbying capability across the border. It is baffling how Hong Kong could form an intelligent response to major events on the Mainland, say the death of Deng Xiaoping, or to smaller, more mundane activities on the other side of the border, such as cars stolen from Hong Kong.[2] Each country and territory in Asia, big or small, has a China policy. Hong Kong

[2] Car theft and smuggling from Hong Kong into mainland China (Guangdong province) reached a peak in 1994.

does not. Worse still, Hong Kong policy makers pretend to know more about China than others in Hong Kong do.

'China watching' in Hong Kong is dominated by commentators whose first-hand experience of mainland China is twenty years out of date and who choose not to renew their perceptions by going to the Mainland. The Hong Kong civil service is similarly insular. Hong Kong could have been saved from many traumas in the early stages of the transition, if civil servants had managed to put aside their prejudices and accepted the idea of a changing, and, by and large, progressing mainland China. Perhaps the magnitude of these on-going developments—changes in government policies on all fronts, in outlooks and aspirations, in life-styles and, above all, in economic structure and performance levels was too drastic to comprehend, let alone be factored into the transition.

Noone, for example, would have imagined in the late 1980s that Hong Kong developers and other smaller investors would have diverted their overseas real-estate funds from Canada, Australia, and other Western countries into mainland China. Most major developers based in Hong Kong have set aside 10 per cent of their total assets for mainland projects, ranging from housing estates to shopping centres and large office blocks. Smaller investors also flock into the Mainland, notably into Guangdong, to buy up the tens of thousands of residential units churned out by Hong Kong and the mainland developers. Advertisements to sell those units cover pages of Hong Kong newspapers every day.

To make it happen, Hong Kong developers move in with their Hong Kong professionals—architects, project managers, engineers, estate agents, solicitors, property managers, researchers, and accountants. Suppliers of building materials and service installations follow suit. Everybody who wants to stay in these industries and professions has to look north and go north. For the first time in fifty years, and that is the first time in the lives of many Hong Kong professionals, we are working side by side with our mainland counter-parts and learning to deal face to face with the various levels of Chinese government. An informal survey has shown that, in terms of fee income, 40 per cent of local architects' jobs are on the Mainland, stretching into the remote interiors.[3]

---

[3] This is an estimate by the President of the Hong Kong Institute of Architects.

These Hong Kong professionals working on the Mainland, raise another spectre: reciprocity. When the Basic Law was being drafted, professionals in Hong Kong were wary of their mainland counterparts snatching their rice bowls when Hong Kong becomes part of 'one country' in 1997. Article 142 of the Basic Law therefore stipulates, among other things, the following:

> The government of the Hong Kong Special Administrative Region shall, on the basis of maintaining the previous systems concerning the professions, formulate provisions on its own for assessing the qualifications for practice in the various professions. . . . The government of the Hong Kong Special Administrative Region shall continue to recognize the professions and the professional organizations recognized prior to the establishment of the Region, and these organizations may, on their own, assess and confer professional qualifications.

No one imagined at the time, that long before 1997, Hong Kong professionals would be getting a lion's share of the mainland market. No one knows for sure how much longer we can resist the calls for reciprocity, for mainland practitioners to work in Hong Kong. What would back up the Hong Kong argument? Where does our political strength lie on the Mainland?

Potential competition, which is entirely healthy, will not be limited to job opportunities. Continuous progress on the Mainland will bring about, on the positive side, more job opportunities for Hong Kong people, and on the not so positive side, pressure on income differentials. Typically, a Hong Kong graduate would, with a joint-venture employer on the Mainland, command a ten-fold income differential when compared with his mainland equivalent. It has been said that up to 70 per cent of our graduates from some courses in our tertiary institutions are now so employed on the Mainland.[4] Whatever our sentimental feelings, this cold fact remains: the income differential gives some Hong Kong people living standards that we have so far taken for granted. To maintain Hong Kong's competitiveness, its income levels and living standards, not to mention its overall usefulness, Hong

[4] This is an estimate by the Dean of the Faculty of Engineering of the Hong Kong Polytechnic.

Kong people will have to be quick off the mark, identifying and filling new niches in China's economic development.

Still on the subject of real estate, the purpose of Hong Kong's purchases of housing units on the Mainland is not entirely clear. Definitely some are for speculative gains, others to relish in the satisfaction of ownership. Yet others buy as holiday and retirement houses. This is a further change in attitude, and again an unexpected one, from the days of the drafting of the Basic Law. At this time there were serious suggestions that the borders of the Hong Kong SAR should be defined in detail in the Basic Law, just in case the New Territories became part of Shenzhen.

Whatever the motivations of individual purchasers, the Hong Kong Housing Society announced earlier this year that it is studying the feasibility of building and selling low-cost apartments in Shenzhen to able-bodied Hong Kong retirees, in order to release this part of the Hong Kong housing stock and to improve the living conditions of their target purchasers.

The flow of people between Hong Kong and the Mainland is very much two-way traffic. The Hong Kong tours now bring hundreds of Guangdong tourists into Hong Kong every day. With organization for similar group tours underway in Tibet, Hong Kong people will soon rub shoulders with Tibetan tourists in Ocean Park and in the Tsimshatsui shopping centres. The limit on the number of mainland residents given permission to settle in Hong Kong has been raised to over a hundred a day. Major corporations are now employing staff from the Mainland to curb manpower shortage. All these changes are taking place independently of the sovereignty issue. Neither the Joint Declaration nor the Basic Law provides for them. Indeed, they were probably not anticipated by the authors of those two documents.

The human interface will continue to broaden and intensify, culminating in more inter-marriages, or extra-marital and non-marital relationships. The border will be intact, the two systems will remain different, but people will mix and match as they see fit.

The 1990s also marks the dawn of a new era of economic synergy between Hong Kong and the Mainland. The scale of Hong Kong's traditional manufacturing industries relocating to, and then expanding in, Guangdong is well illustrated by the size of the labour force employed in the province, which now numbers about three million. But that was Phase 1. Phase 2, which is just beginning, is when Hong Kong manufacturers combine their capital and their management and marketing expertise with mainland technology and materials. Instead of just producing more of the same kinds of products at lower costs to cover larger markets, Hong Kong now manufactures products such as refrigerators, air-conditioners, rubber tyres, and pharmaceuticals, which were never part of the Hong Kong manufacturing scene. Similarly, Hong Kong's external economy now includes orchards, fisheries, dairy farms, and chicken ranches. Quite apart from the financial returns that these ventures will provide Hong Kong investors, Hong Kong and the Mainland are now more reliant on one another.

The evolving trade, investment, and economic relationships between Hong Kong and the Mainland are revealing the possibility of competition. With economic growth in Guangdong come two threats to Hong Kong's water supply based at Dong Jiang. The first is pollution of water sources and the other—a great deal more difficult to handle—is the demands of the increasingly affluent local population. How patient will the million residents in Shenzhen remain in coping with water rationing when water, 70 per cent from Dong Jiang, runs free to fill bathtubs and wash cars in Hong Kong.

Already Hong Kong has been competing and paying a higher price for Chinese delicacies, ranging from Shanghai hairy crabs to dried abalones. The homes of the Shanghai hairy crabs in the lakes of eastern China are surrounded by tens of millions of mainland residents, who have an equal craze for these crustaceans. Without the add-on costs in Hong Kong, where they are priced at HK$200 a catty, the open-market price of the crabs at their place of origin is RMB30 (about HK$33). We could not have predicted that local residents would have had the money to outbid Hong Kong gourmets. These changes were again not expected, nor could the Joint Declaration negotiators or Basic Law drafters have done anything about them.

The scale and nature of mainland investments in Hong Kong has caught many observers by surprise. In June 1979, a site at the Wanchai reclamation project was bought from the Hong Kong government by China Resources for the construction of the head office building of this largest state-owned conglomerate. The acquisition, albeit at a concessionary premium, was heralded as the most obvious guarantee offered by the Chinese government to maintain Hong Kong's status quo beyond 1997, because, analysts noted, China could have waited until 1997 and taken the whole of Hong Kong for free. Similar logic was again applied to the purchase in August 1982 of a site in Murray Road for the new Bank of China headquarters, at a price of HK$1 billion. Both transactions were considered to carry political overtones.

Today, investments in the Hong Kong real-estate market, directly or indirectly controlled by mainland companies or authorities, constitute the largest overseas source of funds. Nearly all the companies operating in Hong Kong that are ultimately owned by a mainland corporation or authority have a stake in local real estate. A small city on the Pearl River Delta would own, through locally registered companies, typically up to a few billion dollars worth. Overall mainland ownership is believed to be between 3 to 5 per cent of the total real-estate value of Hong Kong. It is not surprising to see mainland companies with a strong following of bankers, real-estate agents, architects, and other professionals, all currying business favours. What is surprising is the disinclination so far on the part of the Chinese government to use this business following for political ends.

Sino-British relations have also changed. Both the nature and the extent of the downturn in the relations were unexpected. In the two years of serious and sometimes fierce negotiations, it was apparent that both sides were hopeful of resuming cooperation as soon as the main argument over sovereignty was over. The two sides should have been able to work closely, to mutual benefit, in the transitional period. The problem, so both sides perceived, would not be between them, but the level of confidence the Hong Kong and international communities had in them. There were even quiet aspirations on the part of some Chinese officials that the British government would seek, train, and put in place Hong Kong residents who would then qualify, under the Basic Law, to form the SAR government and legislature.

The Chinese side is also understood to be quietly accept-
ing the ongoing contributions of so-called 'pro-British' members of the administration of Hong Kong. Much has been
said about the 'through train' concept, which is an analogy
of the provision in paragraph 6 of the 'Decision of the National
People's Congress on the method for the Formation of the
first government and the First Legislative Council of the Hong
Kong SAR':

> If the composition of the last Hong Kong Legislative
> Council before the establishment of the Hong Kong
> Special Administrative Region is in conformity with the
> relevant provisions of this Decision and the Basic Law
> of the Hong Kong Special Administrative Region, those
> of its members who uphold the Basic Law of the Hong
> Kong Special Administrative Region of the People's Republic
> of China and pledge allegiance to the Hong Kong Special
> Administrative Region of the People's Republic of China,
> and who meet the requirements set forth in the Basic
> Law of the Region may, upon confirmation by the
> Preparatory Committee, become members of the first
> Legislative Council of the Region. . . . The term of office
> of members of the first Legislative Council of the Hong
> Kong Special Administrative Region shall be two years.

In the early stage of the transition, the possibilities to be
explored covered not just the 'through train', but the passengers, drivers, guards, bells, and whistles too. Equally, when
relations subsequently became acrimonious, the derailment
was more extensive than the train itself.

Here again, the present scenario is completely at odds with
earlier expectations. Instead of the two governments working together to maintain the spirit and confidence in Hong
Kong, the reality is that the confidence level is at a record
high despite the soured relations between the two countries!

Hong Kong has changed, mainland China has changed,
Asia also has changed. Asia, particularly, South-east Asia where
we live in today, is calmer, more stable, and more prosperous than in the early 1980s. Armed conflicts and civil strife
have largely disappeared. At times, it is regarded as the growth-
engine for the world's economy. There is definitely a lot more
inter-regional economic activities, from trade to tourism, from
passive investment to active manufacturing. Unexpectedly,

our Asian neighbours have been far more supportive, in both moral and substantive terms than some of our distant friends. Whilst Hong Kong has maintained its cosmopolitan charm, and there is now a larger number of Asian people, not just at the Kai Tak airport, but in the schools, workplaces, and the residential neighbourhoods.

Above all, the world has changed. The 'USSR' and the 'Eastern Bloc' have become terms of the past. For Hong Kong people, the most practical lesson from the disintegration of the Soviet Union and the resultant chaos lies not in the strengths and weaknesses of socialism, but in the prioritization of political and economic reforms. Against this backdrop, mainland China is seen in a different light.

For us in Hong Kong, the new world order is not only about the end of the Cold War. It is about the end of the Cold War with China emerging, in more and more ways, as a power to be reckoned with. China will try, or be forced, to be less submissive, and to conduct foreign relations on more equal terms—something she has never done ever since the West came to the East two centuries ago. China could be regarded as a huge market, or a trade partner with too high a trade surplus; she could be a stabilizing force, a friendly power-broker in the international community, or an ideological opponent. She could also be the clearing-house of overseas Chinese networking, or the source of nationalistic influence. The world will not stand idle, whenever a page is turned. Whether it is nuclear armament of North Korea or MFN (most favoured nation status) in the United States, an open China will find itself on the world stage, at times together with Hong Kong.

Since 1984, many copies of the Joint Declaration and later of the Basic Law have been put in air-tight time-capsules, some even filled with inert gases, and put beneath the foundations of many new buildings in Hong Kong. But the transition itself is not so encapsulated. Nor could it take place in a fossilized date-sealed environment of 1984. For all the 'no change' statements that have been written into the Joint Declaration and the Basic Law, and for all the feeling about these historic deeds at the time—whether they were the result of confidence or fear, trust or distrust, colonialism or nationalism—the world about Hong Kong and the world around

Hong Kong has changed to make the transition much better and easier than expected.

The fate of Hong Kong, after all, is determined not only by strokes of pens, or proclamations, or clever political posturing. The forces at work are much greater than these.

10 The Implementation of the Joint Declaration: An Overview

CHRISTOPHER PATTEN

HONG KONG is approaching a threshold unique not only in its own history, but in the history of the world. The success of its passage will depend on many things; but on none more than a clear understanding of the challenges ahead, and of how best to meet them. That understanding can only come through the kind of thorough and uninhibited debate which Hong Kong applies so effectively to every new challenge it encounters. This series of lectures exemplifies that tradition and has already enlightened the debate. I am grateful to you, Vice-Chancellor, for inviting me to add my voice to those of my distinguished fellow lecturers over the last few weeks.

No institution has given more to Hong Kong, over so long, than this University. From the day it opened its doors eighty-two years ago—indeed before then through its precursor the Hong Kong College of Medicine, which itself had some distinguished graduates—it has been turning out young men and women who have become the leaders of our community, the builders of our future. No less than twenty-one members of the Legislative Council, five members of the Executive Council, and eight Secretaries of Hong Kong government Policy Branches are either alumni of the University or members of its staff. Last year's graduates will be among their successors, helping to lead Hong Kong into the twenty-first century.

We know this because, like the generations before them who have passed through this campus, they have learned during their time here that there is nothing more powerful than the power of ideas. The power that is decided, ultimately, not by physical superiority, nor by who has more battalions. The power that comes instead from the mind, tuned—in the words of one graduate of the College of Medicine—to the trend in world affairs, and to the urgent needs of the community. It is a truth which much of the world has had to rediscover during the lifetime of this university: that though the gun, in the hand of the tyrant or, more often, his secret policemen, may win some illusory battles, the mind and the human spirit which animates it, triumphs in the end. There may for a while be darkness at noon. But the sun always breaks through the clouds.

Universities depend on the uninhibited expression of ideas, and the tussle between them. Vice-chancellors around the world know that academic freedom is indivisible. That you cannot say, if you want a healthy university, 'free expression's fine for chemistry or mathematics, but here in the humanities there are unfortunately one or two ideas we must fence off, one or two no-go areas'. As soon as you do that, the no-go areas spread and, behind a fine Potemkin façade, the university dies.

That, too, has had to be rediscovered. I was alarmed to come across recently a statute from my own Alma Mater, the University of Oxford in the County of Oxfordshire. It reads: 'Bachelors and Masters of the Arts who do not follow the philosophy of Aristotle are subject to a fine of five shillings for each point of divergence.'

At the risk of incurring a fine from the Oxford Proctors for an approach which owes more to Plato than to Aristotle, let us look further at the concepts, set out in the Joint Declaration, which embody the essence of Hong Kong. Freedom of expression is certainly one. But there is another, equally important, and that is Hong Kong's 'high degree of autonomy', the idea so eloquently encapsulated in the words of 'one country, two systems'.

As has been said many times, 'one country, two systems' is a visionary idea, and the key to Hong Kong's continued success. But, as with all visionary ideas, many detailed questions need to be answered before it can be put into practice, faithfully translated into every aspect of our daily lives. Our task as we implement the Joint Declaration is to provide those answers, to work out together what autonomy actually means on the ground: for the civil servant, for the captain of industry or finance, for the judge and the lawyer, for the journalist and the editor. For the man or woman who drives the tram, for the housewife, and for the children of

Hong Kong who will inherit the consequences of the answers we provide—especially for the children. Hong Kong's 'high degree of autonomy' is more than an abstract formula arrived at between diplomats across the baize table. Far more than that. It is the very real template for the lives and livelihoods of six million people.

Of course, autonomy is not, in itself, a new idea. Not for Hong Kong, because, as a previous speaker has pointed out, Hong Kong under British sovereignty has long enjoyed a high degree of autonomy. We have never, in the modern era, been told from London how to run our economy, what kind of life we should lead, or how to house and educate ourselves. Some might even argue that the United Kingdom has a thing or two to learn itself from the way we do some of those things. And Hong Kong has, for years, participated fully and autonomously in international trade. It is a valued independent contracting party to the GATT. It is well respected in many other international economic organizations. So there is nothing strange about doing things our way and in our own right.

Nor is autonomy—different systems under the same flag —particularly unusual elsewhere. Despite the wail of bagpipes which occasionally wafts south across Hadrian's wall, Scotland's autonomous legal and educational systems have made the United Kingdom more not less stable, better able to build a society which is more than the sum of its component cultures and traditions. The United States, Germany, and Switzerland have drawn strength, unity, and national pride from the deliberate nurturing of regional autonomy. And in many places, in Europe for example, including the United Kingdom, there is a new tide carrying the making of decisions away from bureaucrats in capitals, and towards the people in the regions who have to live with those decisions. As societies become more modern, more complex, that kind of sensitivity to local circumstances makes more and more sense. So autonomy is not a threat to anyone's sovereignty, but a source of vitality.

There is in this an important lesson for Hong Kong. A lesson which is not always well understood. Hong Kong's autonomy is not something new and mysterious, to be handed over in swaddling clothes at midnight on 30 June 1997. It is, and always has been, part of our lives. We wear it with confidence and we owe much of our success to it. Indeed, we take it for granted that most of the decisions which shape the livelihood of Hong Kong people are taken by Hong Kong people, for Hong Kong people, after open debate in Hong Kong.

Of course, there are some areas which have been and will always be the responsibility of the sovereign power. In those areas, Hong Kong people enjoy, and will continue to enjoy, the right to express themselves frankly, but not the right of final decision. And just as we must be confident about what we can decide on our own, so must the sovereign power. Autonomy means that we can run our own lives, but equally it dictates that we should not try to run the lives of others.

So what exactly is the responsibility towards Hong Kong of those sovereign powers—the signatories of the Joint Declaration—a mere 1,173 days from 1 July 1997? First let me clear up once and for all two misconceptions.

First, there is sometimes a tendency—it has been alluded to by a previous lecturer—to see Britain and China as jealous and uncaring parents squabbling over Hong Kong, in the role of the innocent and injured child. Whilst it is sometimes all too tempting to see oneself as the victim of forces beyond one's control, I do not think that this is a helpful or realistic metaphor—any more so than that of the oft-quoted, oft-kicked, three-legged stool.[1]

It is deeply insulting to Hong Kong, which as we all know is in many ways as advanced as any community in the world, to portray it as a child. And it is absurd to argue that, if we find we have to disagree with our Chinese colleagues about some issue of importance to Hong Kong, we are somehow disregarding Hong Kong's interests. It is because we believe Hong Kong's interests to be worth standing up for that we do sometimes have to differ over how best to interpret and implement the commitments made in the Joint Declaration. But no one questions the aim of the exercise: that Hong

---

[1] 'Three-legged stool' is a metaphor deployed by the Chinese to depict what they see as an erroneous relationship of equality between Britain, China, and Hong Kong. China claims that matters affecting Hong Kong are for discussion by China and Britain alone.

Kong should remain the most dynamic city in the Asia Pacific region, with its way of life, its freedoms, its legal system, its social organization untouched by the change of flag. That is so patently in the best interests of all concerned. Nor is there any disagreement that the Joint Declaration provides the best way of achieving this.

The second misconception is based on the fact that, because recently there has been disagreement on one important issue, somehow the Joint Declaration has gone off the rails. It is assumed by the purveyors of this view that our failure to agree on the arrangements for the last series of elections under British sovereignty somehow implies the failure of the Joint Declaration itself and the erosion of the commitments enshrined in it. The Joint Declaration says only that the Legislative Council will be constituted by elections, not how those elections will be organized (though it would be surprising if the signatories had in mind elections which were not fair and open). It does not address—nor would it have been easy to address, back in 1984—the detailed arrangements for those elections. Moreover, the Joint Declaration certainly does not say that when the contracting parties disagree on any single issue, they must suddenly disagree on everything else.

Think what it is we are trying to achieve. A peaceful transfer of sovereignty, between two powers with vastly different cultures on opposite sides of the globe, is unusual enough. Take into account that the territory in question is no longer Palmerston's largely barren island, but the throbbing metropolis around us today with a per capita GDP exceeding that of Britain, and a total GDP just over a fifth of China's: an economic giant in its own right. Remember that the system we have all agreed to preserve is in many respects fundamentally different from that of the incoming sovereign power (and in other ways, be it noted, different from that of the departing one). Is it really any wonder that there are sometimes disagreements? That sometimes, even, a little crockery gets thrown? Of course not.

But it simply does not follow that the Joint Declaration itself is flawed or weakened. Disagreements and the competition of ideas are an inevitable part of administering a complex society, let alone steering it towards a change of sovereignty. When we have a heated debate here in Hong Kong about some issue internal to Hong Kong, we do not throw up our hands and say 'this is the road to confrontation on everything'. It is through debate, sometimes vigorous debate, as John Stuart Mill knew, that we arrive at the right answers.

Far from being weakened, the principles embodied in the Joint Declaration have in fact emerged, from ten testing years, solid and intact. During those years, there have been those who said that, by now, Hong Kong would be on its knees: that confidence in the future would have evaporated, investors would have taken themselves and their money to Singapore or Shanghai, our future talent—including the brightest graduates of this university—emigrated to Canada or Australia.

Has it happened? Ask the Financial Secretary. Another year of over 5 per cent growth—making possible another budget which cut taxes, raised spending, and increased our reserves. Violent crime falling, when the gloomy men with sandwichboards predicted that it would go through the ceiling. I think the Joint Declaration has so far done a pretty good job of preserving Hong Kong's stability and prosperity.

Of course, that does not mean that we can sit back and congratulate ourselves. The real test is just beginning. There is still an awful lot to do before 1997; and that will only take us to the end of the first chapter: the rest of the book will be written thereafter.

It is for those subsequent chapters that we must and are planning. Let me say in passing that we will be greatly helped in that task by the thorough and thoughtful report published yesterday by the House of Commons Foreign Affairs Committee.[2] I recommend it as required reading for anyone with an interest in our affairs. The Committee took detailed evidence from all parties involved, including the British and Chinese governments, as well, of course, as here in Hong Kong. I am delighted that the section on Hong Kong firmly endorses the approach we—the British government and the Hong Kong government—have taken over the last couple of years, particularly delighted as the report is unanimous and

[2] 'Relations between the United Kingdom and China in the period up to and beyond 1997', published on 23 March 1994.

cross-party. I know that the British government—with the Hong Kong government—will consider very carefully and fully the recommendations which the Committee make.

Let me say a word or two, though, about the kind of priorities which I believe we should now be setting ourselves.

To start with, we need to do far more to ensure the continuity of our laws, and of our legal system. Hong Kong owes so much to its laws and to the rule of law, in which the freedoms and way of life guaranteed in the Joint Declaration are embedded and before which all citizens are equal. It is thanks to the certainty and stability provided by our legal system that Hong Kong has prospered as a place of international trade and finance. There are currently nearly 700 US companies established in Hong Kong; sixty-two more came here in 1993. Why? Hong Kong is after all not the only point of access to the growing markets of East Asia. Companies are coming here because we can offer, more than anywhere else, a level playing field kept level by fair laws effectively and impartially enforced.

We need to keep that competitive edge, that capacity to attract international business—not only to trade with and invest in China (though that is of course vital) but also as a base for wider regional activities, from which to respond to new opportunities as they arise. To take a topical example, Hong Kong is the natural gateway to a rapidly developing Vietnam (where, unsurprisingly, no one has been quicker than our own investors to knock on the doors which are now opening). We need to keep reminding those interested in entering this and other regional markets that there can be no better springboard than Hong Kong.

We shall only succeed in this if we can ensure that the integrity and credibility of our legal system cross the threshold of 1997 without a blemish. That means, for example, demonstrating clearly, well before 1997, not only that, as the Joint Declaration promises, the system of English common law will remain unchanged, but that the body of law which currently applies must also remain in force.

Like much of the business of the Joint Liaison Group (JLG), this requires a lot of dry and unglamorous work. But let no one be misled by that. It is also vital work. There are at present over three hundred UK laws whose application has been extended to Hong Kong. They cover areas as diverse as civil aviation, shipping, commercial arbitration, and copyright. Areas where we—where Hong Kong, where China—cannot afford gaps, ambiguities, or holes in the playing field. Areas vital for our continued success. Left to themselves, these laws would lapse on 1 July 1997: no court in the Special Administrative Region is going to enforce UK legislation. We therefore need before then to replace most of them—those which are not obsolete—with equivalent local legislation.

We also need to adapt most of the 600 or so ordinances and 1,000 items of subsidiary legislation already on our own statute book, so that they are in a form clearly consistent with the Basic Law, and will therefore (under its terms) continue to apply after the transition. This is partly a technical matter, for example, of replacing the word 'Governor' with 'Chief Executive'. But there are also more complex issues to be resolved, like how to align the provisions in the Immigration Ordinance on right of abode with those in the Basic Law.

Let me repeat: this is not just more employment for our numerous and well-nourished lawyers. It is a crucial part of Hong Kong's superstructure. So far, we have, through the JLG, reached agreement with China on the localization of just thirty ordinances. The Chinese side are considering our proposals on some seventy-five other UK enactments, as well as on thirty ordinances to be adapted. They have been studying some of our proposals for up to three years. There is therefore an enormous amount of work to get through. So I make this appeal to our Chinese colleagues. Let us redouble our efforts. We now need, urgently, to speed up this work if we are to finish it in time, and avoid damaging, confidence-sapping gaps in the law.

Then there is our court system itself. At present, the final appeal court in Hong Kong is the Judicial Committee of the Privy Council. The Joint Declaration and the Basic Law state that the SAR will have a Court of Final Appeal based in Hong Kong. This is a significant change that will affect the whole of the legal system. The government, with the strong support of the Chief Justice, believes that, to ensure continuity in 1997, we should attempt to establish the Court well before that date; and we secured Chinese agreement to this in 1991. Most of you will be aware that the agreement we reached with the Chinese side did not find favour with the Legislative Council and with the legal profession in Hong Kong; and that this has so far held up the establishment of the Court. We now need to find a way forward. It is self-evidently in the interests of Hong Kong for the Court to be up and running before 1997. It would be irresponsible for the Hong Kong government not to do everything possible to achieve this, despite the obvious difficulties.

We have therefore now prepared the necessary draft legislation, and we intend to consult both the Chinese side and the legal profession on this before we introduce it into the Legislative Council. It remains based on the agreement reached in 1991, which we continue to believe is the best agreement available. We will spare no effort to convince legislators, and the community, that the way forward which we are proposing represents the only sensible option.

If we fail in this, the Court will have to be established by the SAR itself. This would take time, certainly a year, probably more. We would have to discontinue appeals to the Privy Council at least a year before 30 June 1997, because that is the lead time for appeals to be heard, and we must avoid the legal complications that would occur if a case were in the process of being heard at that date. So we are looking at a potential vacuum of at least two or three years at the highest level of our judicial system, with all the uncertainty which that would create, for Hong Kong people and international investors alike. That is why we need to press ahead now.

There is another matter to which I and my senior colleagues in government attach fundamental importance. That is the civil service. The civil service is the backbone of Hong Kong's administration. The commitments made in the Joint Declaration and in the Basic Law rightly reflect this. I welcome the assurances which Chinese officials have repeatedly given about the need to maintain the morale and efficiency of the civil service. We need to begin discussing soon the practical measures which will be necessary to achieve this, not least on the question of principal officials and continuity of appointments. We are ready to work with the Chinese side to ensure that Hong Kong continues to benefit from a dedicated, impartial, and efficient civil service, imbued with the principles of good clean government and minimum intervention which have made Hong Kong so special. This is an objective which is well within our grasp, if we reach out for it together.

There are of course many other issues on which the sovereign powers will need to work together in the next few years, issues on which no one has anything to gain from failure to agree; and all—but above all the people of Hong Kong—will be the winners from agreement. Some of the issues are familiar to us all. I am glad that we are now again discussing the financial arrangements for Hong Kong's new airport, which Hong Kong so obviously needs, but which also will bring enormous benefits to South China.

I am also glad that this week we were able to carry forward discussions with the Chinese side on immigration and right of abode issues. These are rightly of great interest to the community. The question of who will be entitled to enjoy the right of abode in the Territory after 1997 affects people both of Chinese and non-Chinese origin. If the JLG were to fail to reach clear-cut conclusions on this important issue, some members of our community would face real uncertainty about their future here. Similarly it is important for the JLG to reach conclusions about the preservation of existing arrangements for visa-free travel overseas. Ease of travel overseas is a convenience which Hong Kong people rightly enjoy; it also facilitates trade and tourism and therefore makes an important contribution to Hong Kong's prosperity.

Although there are recognizable sensitivities for the future sovereign power in some of these issues, the vital consideration is that both the Chinese and British sides owe it to Hong Kong to make early progress over them in order to put in place the necessary arrangements well before 1997.

Similarly we are negotiating agreements with a number of countries to enable Hong Kong to return fugitive criminals to their country of origin, and to get back criminals who flee from Hong Kong. These agreements play an important role in the fight against international crime. If they are to remain valid after 1997 they must be cleared through the JLG. If they are not all in place by 1997, our ability to fight international crime will be impaired and Hong Kong risks becoming a haven for criminals.

I referred earlier to the new airport. An important component in Hong Kong's future prosperity is the preservation of its civil aviation regime, as provided for in the Joint Declaration. In the JLG, we are negotiating a network of air services agreements between Hong Kong and key aviation partners to extend beyond 1997. We have already reached agreement on some. There are still a substantial number of initialled agreements under consideration in the JLG, and others still for negotiation. If we are unable to complete this programme, the effectiveness of Hong Kong's existing civil aviation relationships will suffer, as will Hong Kong's reputation as a major centre of international civil aviation.

All in all, there remains much to be done. It is encouraging that last month the Chinese Foreign Minister stated that, whatever our differences on the constitutional issue, cooperation in the Joint Liaison Group and over the airport would not be affected. I welcome this. It accords entirely with our view. I am glad, for example, that an agreement on the future of the British military estate in Hong Kong now looks within reach.

More broadly, I am glad that the flourishing cross-border relationship is contributing so much not only to Hong Kong, but also to our neighbours in Guangdong. I am sure we will need to do our best to answer other questions which will only become apparent later on. But whatever the issue, we will continue to work night and day to achieve agreement, wherever it is in the interests of Hong Kong.

In the end, when the twenty-eighth Governor of Hong Kong is long departed, when the first Chief Executive of the Hong Kong Special Administrative Region has come, and when he or she has gone for that matter, it will be Hong Kong people here in Hong Kong who will have to digest the fruits of our labour.

I am sometimes invited to prophecy what I think Hong Kong will be like, say, ten years from now, twenty years into the Joint Declaration. But prophecy is dangerous, unless done retrospectively! It is all too easy to get carried away, like the Director-General of the Zambian National Academy of Space Research, who in 1964 reportedly promised the World: 'I will have my first Zambian astronaut on the moon by 1965'. So listen instead, as it is always worth listening, to Sir Karl

Popper, who reminds us that 'We may become the makers of our fate when we have ceased to pose as its prophets.'

The point is, we cannot just sit back and rely on history to shape our future. History doesn't work like that. History is not made by the north wind, nor by any other remote forces beyond our control. Tomorrow's history will be the chronicle of our actions today. We write it ourselves, and before its implacable court we bear the responsibility for what we write.

So we all—the governments of Britain and China, the Hong Kong government and, yes, the people of Hong Kong—are responsible for the destiny of Hong Kong. We all have work to do. If we do it together, and do it well, there is almost no limit to what Hong Kong can achieve, poised as it is on the crest of the economic wave surging through East Asia.

But if the Joint Declaration means anything, it is that the achievements of the next century will, like those of this one, be made here in Hong Kong, by you, the people of Hong Kong. And that means, dare I say it, that if the values enshrined in the Joint Declaration are to survive, then Hong Kong people will need to stand up for them and to defend them, even though that may from time to time mean the odd disagreement with the present sovereign power or even conceivably with the future one. For most of the really big decisions over the years have not been taken in Government House, nor even in the chamber of the Executive Council. They have been taken on the streets of Hong Kong, in the markets and boardrooms of Hong Kong, in the meeting places of Hong Kong, and here too on the campuses of Hong Kong. That is what has built our skyscrapers and fed our families. And that, if we succeed, is how it will remain.

DATE DU|

APR 1 4 1997		
MAY 3 1 1997		

UNIVERSITY PRODUCTS, IN